FIX THE U.S. BUDGET!

FIX THE U.S. BUDGET!

*Urgings of an
"Abominable No-Man"*

James C. Miller III

HOOVER INSTITUTION PRESS

Stanford University
Stanford, California

Hoover Institution Press Publication No. 413

First printing, 1994
00 99 98 97 96 95 94   9 8 7 6 5 4 3 2

Manufactured in the United States of America
The paper used in this publication meets the minimum requirements
of American National Standard for Information Sciences—Permanence
of Paper for Printed Library Materials, ANSI Z39.48–1984. ∞

Library of Congress Cataloging-in-Publication Data
Miller, James Clifford.
    Fix the U.S. budget! : urgings of an "abominable no-man" /
James C. Miller III.
        p.   cm. — (Hoover Institution Press publication ; no. 413)
    Includes bibliograhical references and index.
    ISBN 0-8179-9212-X (alk. paper)
    1. United States. Office of Management and Budget.   2. Budget—
United States.   3. Tax and expenditure limitations—United States.
4. Government spending policy—United States.   I. Title.
II. Title: Fix the US budget!   III. Series: Hoover Institution Press
publication ; 413.
HJ2051.M52   1994
336.73—dc20   93-40600
                                                          CIP

This book is dedicated to my father,
James C. Miller, Jr. (1920–1988).

An automobile mechanic, an army air corps veteran of World War II,
a pilot for Delta Air Lines until he retired in 1980,
a civic and church leader, and a family man,
he taught more by example than have legions
of self-appointed guardians of the values of Western civilization.

Daddy, this one's for you!

Contents

List of Figures

Preface

AFTER PARTICIPATING IN THE 1980 ELECTION CAMPAIGN as an adviser and then becoming a member of the Ronald Reagan–George Bush transition team, I joined the new government in January 1981 as an associate director of the Office of Management and Budget (OMB). My task was to help carry through on President Reagan's promise to get the federal government's regulatory apparatus under control—off the backs of businesses and out of the pockets of consumers. We did this by applying straightforward economic analyses to regulatory initiatives and by establishing procedures that prevented agencies from promulgating rules that did not make economic sense. *What* we tried to do was not particularly controversial, at least in the academic community. Legions of regulatory experts had lamented the largely uncontrolled, uncoordinated, and inefficient ways in which federal agencies had promulgated their rules. *How* we went about addressing the problem certainly was controversial. Our approach was to "just say no" to agencies when their proposals didn't make sense. We also required agencies to defend specific rules on the books or else schedule them for termination. This not only generated the ire of the agencies' constituents but precipitated a strong reaction from Capitol Hill. In the view of many members of Congress, this direction from the White House constituted a usurpation of legislative authority.

The reforms took several months to put in place and to begin working in anything like a normal fashion. Thus, having completed what I believed to be the most important part of the effort, I felt free to accept the president's invitation to take over the Federal Trade Commission (FTC) and thus commenced as chairman in October 1981. The FTC was under intense fire from critics—indeed, during 1980 there had been a congressional hiatus that almost resulted in the agency's being shut down. The major problem was that the leaders of the agency had used its elastic statutes to get into areas of social engineering that

Congress had never intended and that even many of the organization's supporters thought were beyond the pale.

Quite simply, the FTC needed to return to basics and, together with a talented senior staff, I sought to carry out that task. I decreed, essentially, that no longer would decisions about what guidance to give industry, what areas to investigate, and what charges to bring be made based on subjective standards of equity (what's fair to me may be unfair to you) but on principles of sound economics consistent with the basic enabling statutes. Also, I set up procedures to ensure that this directive was carried out.

Our efforts at the FTC were controversial, to say the least. Because our early controls resulted in a marked reduction in litigation, the antitrust (and consumer protection) bar rose up in arms, as did the reporters, who saw their stories about the agency's latest antics go from page A-1 to page D-23. Congress, of course, got into the act, with the relevant committees worrying that one of the powerful agencies in their portfolio might not be doing all it could to redistribute economic rents according to committee members' preferences. And finally, the learned professions (doctors, lawyers, et cetera) took a shot at the organization by seeking exemption from its authority. There was never a dull moment. On the whole, however, we won important battles and made significant progress.

After the president's reelection in 1984 and after the FTC reforms had been largely implemented, I began to consider alternatives in the private sector (having promised my family I would serve in the administration only one term). Before I made final arrangements, however, I was offered the job of director of OMB—a position my family readily agreed I couldn't turn down.

Thus, in October 1985 I succeeded David Stockman as budget director and member of President Reagan's cabinet. Stockman had held Washington spell-bound during the first months of the administration—until the now-famous William Grieder article appeared in the *Atlantic Monthly*.[1] During the first year of the new administration, Dave was extremely effective in helping the president restrain spending and cut taxes. Following the appearance of the Grieder piece and his trip to the "woodshed," however, Dave's influence diminished consider-ably, especially on Capitol Hill. Even Dave's subsequent advocacy of a tax *increase* (which the vast majority of Congress supported) did not restore his old clout.

When I took over OMB, members of Congress were looking for someone

---

[1] William Grieder, "The Education of David Stockman," *Atlantic Monthly* 248, no. 6 (December 1981): 27–54. In the article, Stockman is quoted as having no faith in Reaganomics—viewing the program of tax cuts not as supply-side economics but as "trickle-down" economics. Understandably, President Reagan was displeased and gave Stockman a dressing-down in the Oval Office.

with the integrity they felt Dave Stockman lacked.[2] They were also looking for someone who would be "cooperative," especially on spending priorities and taxes. Whether they found in me someone with integrity I'll leave for others to report. But they didn't find someone who would be as cooperative as they had hoped.

One of my predecessors as OMB director, James T. Lynn (now retired chairman of the Aetna Life Insurance Company), once characterized the OMB director as "the Abominable No-Man." To do his or her job, the OMB director has got to say no to crazy ideas, to bad ideas, to so-so ideas, and even to good ideas with low priority. And the flow of such ideas—from Capitol Hill, from officials in the administration, and from the general public—is seemingly endless. I played the role of abominable no-man with particular relish. An early *New York Times* assessment of my performance reported "The Miller Lexicon: No, No, No, No, No" and compared me with Zorro—slashing Ns instead of Zs along the corridors of Capitol Hill.[3]

To me, the abominable no-man role was not only a matter of institutional responsibility but of faithfully carrying out the president's policies. After all, Ronald Reagan had come to Washington bent on cutting taxes and spending and reordering spending priorities to favor defense at the expense of domestic programs. No doubt when Reagan was elected this reflected the public's sentiment as well. But after some initial successes, the president lost a degree of public support and, unfortunately, did little to recover it in the "I'm OK, you're OK" presidential campaign of 1984. Certainly, by the time I returned to OMB, the prevailing view on Capitol Hill was that social programs had been neglected and that spending on them should be increased—financed in part by a reduction in defense spending but mostly by an increase in taxes (usually clothed in the rhetoric of a need to reduce the deficit).

Another compelling reason I opposed increases in both spending and taxes was my training in the economics and political science subdiscipline of "public choice," which made me aware that our current federal decision-making institutions result in excessive levels of both. In a sense, then, my responsibility as a public official was to serve as a brake on the propensity of the federal government to direct ever-larger shares of citizens' resources.

Saying no to spending and tax increases did not make me popular on Capitol Hill. As the public choice literature amply demonstrates, on the whole members of Congress act as though they have a consuming drive to be reelected. They maximize the likelihood of being reelected if they spend on programs that benefit

---

[2] Just before my confirmation, Senator Fritz Hollings volunteered to a national TV audience, "Jim Miller is Dave Stockman with just one set of books."

[3] Jonathan Fuerbringer, "The Miller Lexicon: No, No, No, No, No," *New York Times*, March 13, 1986, p. A24.

their constituents and tax somebody else to pay for them. In particular, members of Congress are desirous of having the OMB director support, or at least acquiesce to, their pet projects, whether it is a matter of including them in the president's budget, authorizing an executive agency to use its discretion to fund them, or recommending that the president sign legislation mandating them.

Members of Congress are not often able to exempt their constituents from overall tax increases, but here they do the next best thing: they blame someone else. Thus, the ideal OMB director, from the congressional standpoint, is someone who will march up to Capitol Hill and with a somber face state categorically that a tax increase is absolutely necessary to balance the federal budget, to maintain economic growth, and, indeed, to assure peace for all. In a variant of Senator Russell Long's (D., La.) dictum, "Don't tax me, don't tax thee, tax that man behind the tree," by and large members of Congress want a tree to *hide behind* when it comes to increasing taxes. In that regard, they saw in me not a mighty oak but an axe-wielding lumberman intent on cutting down every tree they tried to hide behind.

The events described in chapters 2 through 8 reflect this tension between a Congress bent on expanding the size and scope of the federal sector and an administration with the reverse goal in mind. Some of the exposition is autobiographical. My intent is *not* to produce another kiss-and-tell tract but to acquaint the reader with *how* the system works: how it succeeds and, especially, how it fails. As will become evident, I believe the budget system's failures are of sufficient import that steps must to be taken to correct them. In the last chapter I outline what needs to be done if the U.S. budget is to be saved.

Although some members of some institutions will be embarrassed, or at least sensitive, about some of the revelations here, I have taken great pains to protect the guilty as well as the innocent. To repeat, the narrative is meant to inform the reader about how the system works (along with the goals we established and the methods we employed) rather than to sensationalize history.

In addition, I want to convey a sense of what it's like to live life in the fast lane in Washington—or, as Terry Golden, former head of the General Services Administration, put it, life in the *oncoming* lane. Our government depends on people as well as institutions, and an understanding of what motivates them and the environment in which they function may help assess the likely outcome(s) of institutional change. Although anecdotal, my own experience is not atypical, and thus in places I have included a modicum of personal material.

Acknowledgments

Although I am the author and thus bear sole responsibility for any errors this book contains or misjudgments it reflects, a number of people and organizations enabled it to come about or at least made possible some of the events it describes.

First, I want to thank my colleagues at OMB and the FTC, especially the senior staff: Wayne Arny, Terry Baxter, Bob Bedell, Larry Burton, Tom Campbell, Jack Carley, Carol Crawford, Ed Dale, Randy Davis, Bob Dawson, Katheryn Eickhoff, Jeff Eisenach, Wendy Gramm, Larry Harlow, Jennefer Hirshberg, Arlene Holen, Al Keel, Tim Muris, Jay Plager, Judy Pond, Alan Raul, Gerry Riso, Emily Rock, Merrie Spaeth, Debbie Steelman, Bob Tollison, Jim Tozzi, Fred Upton, Ron Utt, Gordon Wheeler, John Weicher, Joe Wright, and last, but certainly not least, Bruce Yandle. In addition, I want to express my admiration for the career staff of those agencies. Year in and year out they perform outstanding work under extraordinary pressure, for extremely long hours, and most at pay levels well below what they could command in the private sector.

Second, I want to note appreciation to my colleagues at Citizens for a Sound Economy (CSE), particularly Rich Fink and Wayne Gable. Their knowledge and perspective on current policy developments have proven most valuable and their enthusiasm, contagious. In addition, I have found the views of the 250,000 members and supporters of CSE a sobering tonic for anyone caught up with life inside the Washington beltway.

Third, I want especially to thank my colleagues at the Center for Study of Public Choice at George Mason University. The intellectual underpinnings of my work in government stem from my longtime association with this group of people and the subdiscipline they have developed (for which James Buchanan won a Nobel Prize in Economics in 1986). Particular mention should be made of the center's director, Robert Tollison, and the other associates at the center, including Roger Congleton, Mark Crain (who graciously spent a year's sabbatical at OMB in 1987–1988), David Levy, Gordon Tullock, and Richard Wagner.

Fourth, I want to express sincere gratitude to the John M. Olin Foundation, whose generous grant to Citizens for a Sound Economy and the Center for Study of Public Choice enabled me to take time to reflect on and write about my recent government experiences. The Olin Foundation has funded the work of a number of scholars interested in public policy, and the world is a better place because of its efforts.

Fifth, I would like to thank the Hoover Institution and its director, John Raisian, for their support of this volume.

Finally, I want to acknowledge the contributions of those many who have helped shape this manuscript—from transcribing materials to checking facts to commenting on drafts to editing text. Particular mention should be made of Annelise Anderson, Patricia Baker, Terry Baxter, Mark Bradford, Janet Byrd, John Cogan, Mark Johnson, Fred Nutt, Jay Rao, Alan Raul, Gary Richardson, Carol Robert, Tom Walton, Ann Wood, and, last but not least, my wife, Demaris.

1 | Antecedents

By THE TIME I TOOK OVER as Ronald Reagan's budget director in October 1985, I had served in his administration for four and a half years and thus had a good idea of the Reagan goals and how to make agencies work to achieve them. I had also gone through a rigorous confirmation process.

White House "regulatory czar"

At the beginning of the Reagan administration I became known as the White House "regulatory czar"—a dubious distinction, considering the fate of Czar Nicholas! My job was to get the regulatory machinery of the U.S. government under control and to improve its effectiveness. If it took acting like a despot to do the job, then so be it!

During the last year of the Ford administration I directed the regulatory review work of the old Council on Wage and Price Stability and was able to observe firsthand the workings (and failings) of federal regulators. From that experience I concluded that, to improve the performance of the regulatory agencies, simply requiring them (or someone else) to perform an economic analysis of their proposals' likely effects was not enough: someone outside the agency needed to be empowered to tell an agency it could not regulate unless its proposals made common (that is, economic) sense.[1] That view received added confirmation as I analyzed Jimmy Carter–era regulatory activity from the vantage of a post at the American Enterprise Institute.

---

[1] See, for example, "Lessons of the Inflation Impact Statement Program," *Regulation*, July/August 1977.

Thus, when asked by Reagan adviser Marty Anderson to serve on the campaign's regulatory task force, I was anxious to do so and to persuade anyone who would listen of the need to install a mechanism to assure compliance with common sense. Given that the raison d'être of regulators is to regulate, they will produce regulations without end—bad ones as well as good ones. The key is to determine which is which and to stop the bad ones. If you tell the agencies they can't regulate *unless* their proposals meet specific criteria, they will alter their behavior. Our regulatory task force issued a report recommending that criteria be established and that someone be empowered to say no to bad rules. [2]

After the election, I served as captain of the transition team for the Federal Trade Commission (FTC). But after turning in the team's report just before Christmas, I was asked to head the final transition on the regulatory reform effort. Thus, in early January, a group of us met at the transition headquarters to discuss what, specifically, should be done to carry out Ronald Reagan's promise to get the regulatory apparatus under control. The group included Mike Uhlmann (subsequently a member of the White House senior staff), Ray Peck (subsequently administrator of the National Highway Safety Administration), and, most notably, Boyden Gray. Boyden had just been selected to serve as George Bush's counsel, and there was some indication that part of the new vice-president's portfolio would be supervising the regulatory reform effort.

Discussions culminated in a general meeting of the minds that someone had to be in a position to tell the regulators no, that this someone needed to be located in the Executive Office of the president, and that we needed to write down as explicitly as possible the set of standards agencies would be required to meet. Thus, someone at the White House would be able to say no *because* the agency hadn't met the stated (commonsense) requirements for its proposed rule.

I took a hand at drafting the standards, and being an economist I naturally thought of ordinary efficiency criteria. The first requirement of the agency was that if it didn't have enough information to determine the effects of its proposal, the proposal could not go forward. Second, if the agency wanted to reach a specific regulatory objective (lower exposure, safer product, or whatever), it should choose the least costly way of meeting that goal. Third, if, after choosing the least costly alternative, the agency couldn't show that the benefits of the rule exceeded the costs, it should go back to the drawing boards.

These principles were agreed to, and after some editing of language Boyden Gray incorporated them into a draft executive order. I took this draft with me to the first day of the new administration, where, as OMB's new associate director in charge of regulatory policy, I hoped to get it signed by the president.

---

[2] Task force members included Murray Weidenbaum (chairman, Washington University at Saint Louis), Paul Oreffice (Dow Chemical), and John Snow (CSX).

It quickly developed that the vice-president would, indeed, lead the regulatory reform effort, with staff assistance from the regulatory division of OMB.[3] On January 22, 1981—the day after the inauguration—the vice-president empaneled a cabinet-level Task Force on Regulatory Relief, and I was appointed executive director (in addition to my other title at OMB). Working closely with Boyden Gray and Rich Williamson (of the White House staff), we recommended that the vice-president press for approval of the executive order as soon as possible. Bush was amenable, and so we set forth to push all the right buttons.

Time was of the essence, as lawyers say, for the executive order—providing that a unit in the White House could stop an agency from issuing a regulation—would be seen as a serious taking of power from the regulatory heads. At the present moment, however, *none* of the major regulatory agencies were led by a Reagan appointee. Each was headed by a civil servant in an acting capacity, and these individuals were not likely to raise a serious alarm.[4] But the danger lay in delaying too long. If the regulatory agencies began to be filled by Reagan appointees, and if these appointees (with encouragement from the bureaucracy and the agency's other constituents) began to feel their oats, it would be difficult, if not impossible, to get the executive order through the approval process.

The first step was to make sure the draft executive order was "bulletproof" —that is, could withstand court challenge. Accordingly, we obtained the advice of the White House Counsel's office and the Office of Legislative Counsel at the Department of Justice. Their assurance of the order's legality was golden: despite reams of rhetoric from critics alleging its unconstitutionality, no challenge to its basic integrity has ever been successful. One reason is that the order clearly indicates that its provisions are relevant only "to the extent permitted by law."

Executive Order 12291 was signed by President Reagan on Tuesday, February 17, 1981. After the Task Force on Regulatory Relief had approved the draft the week before, we circulated copies to members of the cabinet over the weekend.[5] Then, following the vice-president's presentation at a cabinet meeting, the pres-

---

[3] The Paperwork Reduction Action (the last bill signed by President Carter—over the objections of every member of his cabinet, save his budget director, James McIntyre) created in OMB an Office of Information and Regulatory Affairs (OIRA) on April 1, 1981. I was appointed administrator of that office and incorporated within that office the personnel of OMB's regulatory division and the regulatory analysis division of the (terminated) Council on Wage and Price Stability. Although the responsibilities of OIRA reached beyond regulation (to government information policy generally), its principal activity was reviewing proposed rules and analysis under Executive Order 12291.

[4] Indeed, most of them looked to me for policy direction.

[5] Several members of the cabinet complained to us that because it was a holiday weekend they had no lawyers around to review the draft order for them. We were grateful the lawyers took their holiday.

ident signed the order and made regulatory relief an integral part of the program of economic recovery he announced two days later.

The order spells out the following requirements:

1. Administrative decisions shall be based on adequate information concerning the need for and consequences of proposed government action.

2. Regulatory action shall not be undertaken unless the potential benefits to society for the regulation outweigh the potential costs to society.

3. Among alternative approaches to any given regulatory objective, the alternative involving the least net cost to society shall be chosen.

4. Agencies shall set regulatory priorities with the aim of maximizing the aggregate net benefits to society, taking into account the condition of the particular industries affected by regulations, the condition of the national economy, and other regulatory actions contemplated for the future.

These, then, were the requirements the agencies had to meet—so long as doing so didn't violate any existing law.

To check on whether agencies were meeting these requirements, agencies were required to submit a regulatory impact analysis of their major rules (defined as having more than $100 million annual impact on the economy) to my office at OMB, where we would review them and judge whether the regulatory proposals met the criteria set forth in the executive order. If we said no, the decision could be appealed to the Task Force on Regulatory Relief, but usually this didn't happen. First, my office didn't say no unless there was good reason, and, second, most regulators would not risk taking the time of the vice-president and members of the task force to plead for what might seem like a self-serving case.

Of course, we worked with the agencies to define costs and benefits and to work out methodologies for measuring them, in part by issuing OMB circulars. In particular, we worked to develop techniques for dealing with benefit estimates. Some of our sharpest critics alleged that because benefits could not be easily measured, the majority of regulatory proposals would be rejected. We, however, viewed that approach as being as illegitimate as the view that any regulation that conceivably could produce something of value had to be approved, no matter what the cost.

The effects of our new review procedure, combined with the freeze of the "midnight regulations,"[6] were dramatic. The number of pages published annually

---

[6] In the last few days of the Carter administration, regulatory heads had sent to be printed in the *Federal Register* a slew of new regulatory proposals and final rules. Richard Willard,

in the *Federal Register* plummeted, from 87,012 in 1980 to 63,554 in 1981 to 50,998 in 1984. More important, the regulations we did issue were much more thoroughly reviewed and more soundly based than those of previous administrations. For the first time, agency officials knew that they had to give their rules more than lip service; they had to convince a skeptic that, indeed, their proposals did make sense.[7]

Although ready to take on the regulators for what many regarded as a history of excess, I viewed our work in the broader context of its contribution to economic growth. It was supply-side economics in the best sense of the term. That is, to the extent a regulatory agency uses scarce resources and produces something of lesser value in return, it *diminishes* the gross economic product of the country. In contrast, to the extent that, through careful crafting of regulations, an agency produces more value than the resource cost it expends, the country's gross product is increased.

The reduction in uncertainty, of course, served to make business plans plausible, for the new procedures assured businesses that new regulations were likely to be cost-effective and not unduly intrusive. Also, the procedures for publishing the agencies' rule-making *plans*—enabled by Executive Order 12498 (which was issued after I left OMB)—made industry able to cope with what its leaders had previously seen as a disorderly and unpredictable enterprise in the business of delivering a series of costly "hits." No wonder that regulatory relief was just what the doctor ordered.

Chairman of the Federal Trade Commission

During the Reagan-Bush transition, participants were told of a hard-and-fast rule: no one serving on the transition team for a given agency would receive an appointment at that agency. That rule reduced the amount of jockeying that team members might otherwise undertake to secure themselves a job and thus led to more objective analysis and report writing.

---

a lawyer with the White House Counsel's Office (subsequently appointed to be associate attorney general for the Civil Division), pointed out that the new agency heads could withdraw the new rules—even some that had already been published. We prepared, and the president signed on January 19, a memorandum directing agency heads to withdraw these rules for further consideration (and for submission through the OMB review process).

[7] For example, the Occupational Safety and Health Administration's Hazard Communication Standard required manufacturers using hazardous or potentially hazardous chemicals to label such chemicals at every stage in the production process. After this "midnight regulation" was withdrawn, it was modified to be less costly and was subsequently approved.

At the beginning of the new administration there was no vacancy at the FTC. Members have seven-year terms, and although by convention the member serving as chair resigns whenever there is a change in presidents (especially when a Democrat replaces a Republican or vice versa), this is not a requirement. In this case the incumbent chairman (Michael Pertschuk) chose to remain a member of the commission. In April 1981, however, one of the other members (Robert Pitofsky) announced his resignation, opening the way for the president to appoint a new member and name her or him chair.

Despite my having served as captain of the FTC transition team, I was asked to head the FTC. Although flattered, I demurred, citing the unfinished business with the program of regulatory relief. A deal was struck: I would remain with the regulatory relief effort, but I would go over at the end of September, when the term of an incumbent commissioner (Paul Rand Dixon) expired. After nomination and confirmation, I became chairman of the FTC on October 5, 1981.

When I arrived at the FTC, my views and those of my new colleagues were already well known.[8] Moreover, by that time the Reagan administration's approach to regulation was the subject of some controversy, with critics portraying us as mindlessly opposed to all restraints on business. That charge was wide of the mark. Failures often justify regulatory intervention, and, obviously, there's a need for health and safety rules. Regulation is also necessary to prevent fraud, deception, harmful discrimination, and collusion—the type of malfeasance the FTC is responsible for policing. But in the absence of such market failures, free competition is far more likely to serve consumers and the public than any directives handed down by well-meaning bureaucrats in Washington.

Our proper role was *not* to tell entrepreneurs how to run their businesses or to impose our views on consumers in a fit of Big Brotherism. Rather, our role was to keep markets competitive and free of fraud and deception, thus serving the interests of honest tradespeople and consumers alike.

This approach marked a departure from the previous administration, whose FTC leaders were preoccupied with using the agency to achieve their version of social justice. They should have known the FTC was not set up or equipped to be a morality court. When the agency was just ten years old—back in 1924—a prominent legal scholar warned against pious posturing. He suggested the temp-

---

[8] A perspective of our methodology and approach can be gleaned from the selections in Robert J. Mackay, James C. Miller III, and Bruce Yandle, *The Federal Trade Commission: The Political Economy of Regulation* (Stanford: Hoover Institution Press, 1987). A description of some of the changes we brought to the FTC and the reasons for same are found in James C. Miller III, *The Economist as Reformer: Revamping the Federal Trade Commission* (Washington: American Enterprise Institute for Public Policy Research, 1989).

tation would be great because "a crusade is more spectacular than a scientific inquiry and a moral issue has greater political value than a practical adjustment."[9]

The excesses of the late 1970s generated such a backlash that the agency's very life was put in jeopardy. In 1980 Congress shut the agency down for a day, and it took President Carter's personal intervention to get it going again. Of course, some said the FTC had gotten in trouble for doing its job too well. But frittering away taxpayer resources in pursuit of elitist social theories simply didn't sell with the public or with Congress.

In the competition area, the commission had devoted extraordinary resources to unorthodox cases, pressing at the very frontiers of antitrust law. One of my former associates dubbed this "Star Trek law enforcement—boldly going where no man or woman had dared go before!" During the Carter era, the commission lost more than 60 percent of its antitrust decisions on appeal to the federal courts.

The commission's forays into social engineering such as "kid-vid"[10] also were roundly denounced by the vast majority of commentators. Although some continued to protest that the commission was "only doing its job," it stretched credibility to say the entire business community was wrong, that Congress was wrong, and that the public was wrong—that only Ralph Nader and the FTC leaders knew what they were doing. The simple truth was the FTC could not be effective so long as those subject to its authority viewed its activities as beyond the scope of congressional intent and its operating style as more inquisitional than objective.

So one of our first tasks was to change priorities and restore trust in the commission—to eschew moralistic posturing in favor of sober calculation and to address the fundamental question: Is what we're doing truly in the public interest? That is, does it promote competition and consumer welfare? Part of the regime was to follow the physician's creed: First do no harm. We needed to restrain ourselves when some firm came in and claimed its rival was engaged in predatory behavior; it might simply be competition at work. Nor should we be so quick to prevent the dissemination of useful information for fear that someone *might* be deceived, such as when the commission—thinking that consumers would not understand the claims and might be misled by them—prevented advertisements detailing cigarette tar and nicotine content during the 1950s and automobile mileage claims in the early 1970s.

Instead, we devoted our resources to policing business practices that truly harmed competition and injured consumers, such as price-fixing by doctors and

---

[9] Gerald C. Henderson, *The Federal Trade Commission* (New Haven: Yale University Press, 1924), p. 341.

[10] Using the FTC act to force companies *not* to advertise certain products to children over the airwaves—a decision more appropriately left to Congress.

other professionals, mergers that substantially lessened competition, fraud schemes that robbed vulnerable groups of their hard-earned savings, and deceptive practices that harmed honest tradespeople and caused consumers to waste their money.

In our dealings with business, we also sought to become less adversarial, more professional in hopes of securing so-called voluntary compliance as a cost-effective alternative to litigation. We thought success should be measured by the degree to which we got those subject to our laws, rules, and regulations to abide by them—*not* by how often we sued people.

The "sue first–talk later" approach is not only counterproductive but terribly unfair. To be fair and effective, those subject to the FTC authority must understand the rules. And those at the FTC must realize that many times the failure of companies to abide by the rules is due to their ignorance, not malice or greed.

In applying these principles to the day-to-day operations of the FTC, we benefited greatly from the transition report mentioned earlier.[11] That report contained a number of recommendations for the commission, and we were determined to respond to them (after all, we had written them in the first place!)[12] The report recommended that the commission

1. *Concentrate its resources on those horizontal collusion cases[13] where injury is great and where the market will be slow to respond.* We did that. The portion of our antitrust enforcement resources devoted to horizontal restraints rose dramatically.

2. *Evaluate critically . . . and develop [standards for] shared monopoly cases.[14]* The Exxon case was terminated before we arrived, and Kellogg—the cereals matter—was given a merciful death shortly thereafter. No new shared monopoly cases were attempted.

3. *Evaluate critically . . . and develop [standards for] vertical merger and business practice cases.[15]* We pursued no such cases except those posing a danger arising out of horizontal collusion.

---

[11] Senator Howard Metzenbaum inserted a copy of this confidential report in the *Congressional Record* (September 21, 1981), pp. S-10162–69.

[12] Most of the new FTC senior staff had been members of the FTC transition team.

[13] Situations where two or more producers of the same product or service agree on prices and/or other terms of trade.

[14] The notion that concentrated industries can share monopoly power even in the absence of overt collusion.

[15] For example, when a window manufacturer buys a lumber company.

4. *Evaluate critically . . . and develop [standards for] conglomerate merger cases.*[16] We brought no conglomerate merger cases.

5. *Evaluate critically . . . and develop [standards for] horizontal merger cases brought principally on strictly "structural" grounds.*[17] In June of 1982 we issued a statement of principles[18] emphasizing that concentration per se is neither a necessary nor a sufficient condition for the FTC to challenge a proposed merger.

6. *Evaluate critically . . . and develop [standards for] Robinson-Patman [price discrimination] cases.* We were careful not to bring Robinson-Patman cases when the result would be to restrain competition but rather, consistent with current legal opinion, brought cases only when doing so would be consistent with the spirit of the other antitrust laws (for example, as a way of policing horizontal price-fixing).

7. *Terminate all cases based on "social theories" and consider guidelines to staff concerning future proposals.* The children's advertising rule making was effectively terminated by Congress before we arrived, and we informed the staff that forays into social engineering would be looked on with distrust.

8. *Develop a policy protocol declaring unlawful only those advertising practices that deceive ordinary consumers and alter their purchase decisions accordingly.* The commission issued such a statement on October 14, 1983,[19] amid great gnashing of teeth.

9. *Rely more heavily on the monitoring of industry self-regulation and less on the setting of industrywide standards.* We did that, emphasizing the value of industry self-regulation, ranging from acceptable canons of ethics for professional associations to self-regulatory mechanisms in the advertising industry.

10. *Ferret out cases of industry cartelization through occupational regula-*

---

[16] For example, when a manufacturer of TV sets purchases a fast food chain.

[17] That is, where there is little likelihood of collusion, but where the merger—for example, between two steel manufacturers—would result in an unusually high level of consternation in the industry.

[18] *Statement of Federal Trade Commission Concerning Horizontal Merger Policy* (June 14, 1982).

[19] See, for example, my letter to Congressman John D. Dingell of October 14, 1983, reprinted in *Trade Regulation Reporter* (October 31, 1983). Obtaining commission approval of the new protocol proved difficult because some commissioners wanted to retain broad discretion to block advertisements they found unacceptable. I wanted to narrow the discretion and communicate simple rules that advertisers could understand.

tion, but express due concern for considerations of federalism. Our efforts to restrain price-fixing, fraud, and deception in the medical and legal professions were very successful. [20] But in these and other areas we were very conscious of the appropriate scope of federal (vs. state and local) activities.

11. *Analyze imperfections in regulation as well as imperfections in the marketplace.* The staff was cautioned to be thoroughly conversant with the possible adverse consequences of an FTC intervention, just as they were expected to analyze the market imperfections we might be trying to correct.

12. *Evaluate the Line of Business [LB] and Quarterly Financial Report [QFR] programs.* [21] After thorough review, the commission determined that those programs should no longer collect data but should further analyze the data already collected and make it available for research use. The QFR program was transferred to the Department of Commerce.

13. *Emphasize studies of the effects of government activity on the competitive marketplace, particularly the effects of government regulation.* We did this, not only in preparing studies of the adverse impacts of government controls on competition but in guiding resource allocation in both the consumer protection and the competition areas.

14. *Institute a research program dealing with the problems and status of small business.* We prepared numerous studies of interest to small business and also established a small business liaison within the commission.

In addition, the report recommended that

15. *The president should appoint a new chairman from outside the agency.* He did.

---

[20] For example, in *FTC v. Superior Court Trial Lawyers*, the commission concluded that trial lawyers could not strike the District of Columbia government for higher wages. In *FTC v. Indiana Federation of Dentists*, the Supreme Court reversed a lower court, upholding the FTC's determination that a scheme by dentists that led to higher prices violated the antitrust laws.

[21] The LB program required a random selection of companies to report their profits by individual product or service line. The program had been the subject of considerable criticism because the data were considered too subjective and therefore unreliable for use in economic analyses. The QFR program requested extensive information on sales, costs, profits, and other aspects of business questions from a random sample of firms. It was criticized as being irrelevant and implying FTC surveillance.

16. *The base of the agency's corps of administrative law judges [ALJs] should be broadened.* Because there was little attrition among the agency's ALJs, it was not feasible to achieve this objective.

17. *The agency's economists should play a greater role in deciding which initiatives are brought before the commission.* The working relationship between the agency's lawyers and economists improved dramatically. Although the economists did not receive veto power on law enforcement initiatives, they had substantial input at the bureau level and were able to offer independent advice before the commission.

Moreover, the report concluded that the commission should

18. *Develop a program of periodic reviews of ongoing investigations.* Consistent with standards for evidence and due process, the staff was directed to process investigations and complaints more expeditiously. The commission also adopted rules to expedite its own decision making.

19. *Issue a policy protocol or guideline defining the term* unfair *under Section 5 of the Federal Trade Commission Act.* This was accomplished in the form of a letter to Congress during December 1980, before the inauguration.[22]

20. *Increase the size and scope of its program of intervening with other government agencies.* We established an intervention program that prepared extensive comments for other federal agencies and commented on proposals by state and local agencies.

21. *Take steps to integrate the Bureau of Economics with the rest of the agency physically.* Offices for the economic bureau and staff were established in the headquarters building, and headquarters personnel were encouraged to visit the economists in their building.

22. *Improve relations with Congress.* The commission was no longer threatened with a congressionally imposed shutdown. And efforts were made to improve congressional understanding of, and support for, the commission's new agenda—the return to basics.

23. *Develop procedures to assure that the staff observes standards of impartiality.* We carefully observed rules concerning outside contacts and reformed the excessively adversarial, confrontational style that had characterized the commission during the previous administration.

---

[22] See letter from the commission to Senators Wendell H. Ford (D., Ky.) and John C. Danforth (R., Mo.) dated December 17, 1980.

24. *Expand nonlitigation strategies.* We found that business and consumer education—especially in the real estate and credit areas—was most welcome and very successful.

25. *Provide increased guidance to businesspeople.* We expanded our consumer education unit to include a business education component. Extensive efforts here and through the development of protocols and guidelines met with considerable success.

Finally, the report urged the commission to be helpful in getting Congress to

26. *Eliminate the [commission's ten] regional offices.* At the beginning of the Reagan administration there had been considerable emphasis on federalism, and we agreed that because almost every state has its own "little FTC act," expanded roles for states would obviate the need for the FTC regional offices. Prospects for federalism dimmed considerably, however, and after extensive negotiations with Congress a deal was struck to reduce the resources allocated to the FTC's regional offices but to maintain them as effective units.

27. *Terminate the intervenor funding program.* In the past, the FTC had handed out sums to organizations to represent themselves in FTC proceedings.[23] We ended this program.

28. *Reduce the agency's budget [by some 30 percent].* This was accomplished reasonably painlessly and, in light of other reforms, left the agency with ample resources to carry out its statutory mission.

29. *Define the term* unfairness *as contained in Section 5 of the FTC act.* Language defining the term *unfair* along the lines of the protocol issued by the commission before our arrival was contained in the reauthorization bills pending before Congress but have yet to be codified into law.

Thus, out of twenty-nine specific recommendations we accomplished in

---

[23] For example, a consumer organization would be given a contract to represent the interests of consumers in FTC litigation. The program was the subject of much criticism because of the alleged favoritism shown to its militant organizations and the low quality of their work.

major measure at least twenty-five (including one that was completed before we arrived), made substantial progress on two others, and planned to carry out yet another (recommendation #16) at the first opportunity. Closing the regional offices was not possible, for the reasons given. All told, not a bad record for a few years' effort.

2 | **Nomination and Senate Confirmation**

ON JULY 9, 1985, DAVID STOCKMAN RESIGNED as the director of OMB. This did not come as a surprise to me because he had told me a few months earlier that he was planning to leave at the first opportunity. Indeed, Dave had encouraged me to stick around because he was planning to recommend me as his successor. I, however, had promised my family that I would leave government service after the president's reelection and was in the process of arranging for employment in the private sector.

On several occasions, my family and I had discussed what we should do if the president were to offer me a seat at the table (a cabinet post). They supported the idea, even though it would mean longer hours and, in general, more stress and strain.

On several previous occasions there had been a chance I would be tapped for a cabinet post, but it did not materialize. I was considered for secretary of transportation and chairman of the Council of Economic Advisers when these posts opened in 1984, as well as secretary of labor and U.S. trade representative in 1985.

This time, after a whirlwind of press speculation, I was offered the job. On July 18, Don Regan telephoned me with the news from his car, just after visiting with President Reagan at Walter Reed Hospital (where the president was recovering from surgery). It was a moment filled with appreciation, exuberance, and recognition of the profound challenges that lay ahead.

The president nominates cabinet officials, but the Senate gives its advice and (not always) its consent. So my thoughts turned to Senate confirmation. Knowing that Brad Reynolds and Don Devine had both failed to be confirmed, arguably on technicalities, I wanted to be responsive and allow nothing to fall through the cracks, giving no one an excuse to find me unqualified.[1]

Within days, I met with as many members of the Senate Governmental Affairs Committee (the one that would consider my nomination) as possible, all of whom impressed on me the gravity of the task I was about to undertake. I also met with the committee's staff, discussed the hearing process with them, and was given a copy of a formal questionnaire given to all nominees. This extensive document took me several days to complete.[2] I also filled out FBI forms, tax forms, financial disclosure forms, and ethics forms, creating a blizzard of paperwork for my office and for those on the receiving end. I wanted to answer all of these forms truthfully and completely and get them into the appropriate hands as soon as possible, so that nothing would stand in the way of the confirmation process.

The formal nomination papers were transmitted to the Senate on July 31, Congress adjourned for its August recess the next day, and I promptly set about getting ready for my confirmation hearing—which seemed likely to be mid-September—and learning as much about the new job as I could.

Preparing for the Senate hearing

The purpose of a confirmation hearing is to determine whether the president's nominee is fit for the position. I say fit because the old standard of finding one qualified is no longer relevant. What are usually thought of as qualifications—training, knowledge, and experience—no longer suffice for most important political posts; the nominee may also be required to hold "politically correct" views. Moreover, the nominee has to run the gauntlet of the Senate confirmation process, in itself a test of whether the nominee will be tough enough to do his or her job under fire.

From the nominee's perspective, the process is pure hell. First, there is knowing that anything you have ever done in your life can and will be held against you; anything you have written that can be taken out of context is fair game. Almost any charge can be made, and you are virtually helpless to respond

---

[1] Brad Reynolds, the controversial assistant attorney general in charge of civil rights, had been rejected as President Reagan's nominee to be associate attorney general. Don Devine, director of the Office of Personnel Management, had been rejected when President Reagan tried to reappoint him to that post when Devine's term expired. Both rejections had more to do with the policy views of the candidates than with their qualifications.

[2] In fact, it was so extensive, I characterized it to someone as "name every person you have ever met in your life, and if you leave off one name—just one—we've got you!"

to it, for the unwritten, but highly observed, code is that a nominee never speaks to issues before the confirmation hearing. (Woe unto them that do.)

On top of this is the normal anxiety of taking a test. But imagine a test in which the subject is everything you have done in your life. It's an oral exam; you don't know when it will end; and, just to make things interesting, it's broadcast on nationwide TV! It's enough to give anyone the willies.

In the month and a half between the nomination and the confirmation hearing, I tried to meet two objectives. First, to get some rest, we visited former FTC commissioner George Douglas and his wife, Barbara, at their place in the Bahamas. Second, to begin getting ready for the hearing and learning about the job, I brought a good deal of reading material on our two-week vacation.

In mid-August, I had my first briefings at OMB. I met not only with the acting director (Joe Wright) and the senior staff[3] but with the agency's senior career civil servants, many of whom I recognized from my days as administrator of the Office of Information and Regulatory Affairs, back in 1981. I told them that I knew from experience and by reputation that the OMB career staff was the cream of the crop; that, if confirmed, I would look forward to working with them; that I would expect great things from them; and that, in particular, I would expect them to extend to me every courtesy they had shown previous OMB directors in getting me up to speed.[4]

When Congress returned after Labor Day, I scheduled meetings with other members of the committee and with the chairman and ranking members of other budget- or management-oriented committees in the House of Representatives as well as the Senate. Having been forewarned that attempts would be made in private meetings with members of Congress to get me to promise to deliver specific favors or acquiesce to "commitments" allegedly made by my predecessor, I promised only to consider the merits of their proposals once I was confirmed.

At the same time I was preparing for the confirmation hearing, I was carrying on as chairman of the FTC. September is always a busy season for commissioners, and this September was no exception. On top of that, a great deal of winding up needed to be done if I were going over to OMB anytime soon. Specifically, a number of commission decisions had been drafted on matters in which companies

---

[3] OMB then had a director and a deputy director. Reporting to them at the time were various program associate directors—four principally with budget responsibilities, three principally with management responsibilities, and one with responsibilities for both. Two other members of the senior staff had associate director status: the general counsel and the associate director for congressional affairs.

[4] Later, the most senior civil servant related that I would be the seventeenth budget director he had "trained"!

had been sued and in which arguments had been heard before the commissioners sitting as judges. These needed to be resolved.

I wanted to show that I was taking the responsibilities of the FTC chairman seriously for three reasons. First, I wanted to remain in charge and thus get the maximum amount from everyone in pursuing the responsibilities we had before us. Second, an imminent changeover in leadership is a time of great anxiety on the part of an organization's staff. I wanted to keep the staff busy, away from the grapevine and the rumor mill. Third, if I were not taking my job seriously it would have seemed that I felt the OMB confirmation was in the bag.

As the confirmation hearing neared, my pace of preparation accelerated. As is usual with my preparing for a hearing of some sort—especially an oversight hearing—I reviewed a massive amount of information and began discarding that which was less important. By the day of the hearing, I had winnowed a set of material that would fill several filing cabinets down to three folders: (a) responses to the committee (copies of the committee's questionnaires and my responses), (b) top priority (materials I thought I might need to respond to questions), and (c) low priority (materials not likely to be drawn on but available in case they were needed). These all fit nicely into one briefcase.

As the hearing date approached I began to feel more confident that real issues would be addressed and a character assassination avoided. Uniformly, I had received polite treatment from those senators with whom I met, even those whose views differed from mine on important issues. As my confidence grew, the confirmation hearing began to look less like a visit to the dentist and more like a visit to the doctor before going to summer camp: not exactly an enjoyable experience but the price of admission of doing something that is. Nevertheless, at no time did I take the confirmation process lightly.

The Senate also takes its role in the nomination process seriously. According to the Constitution, that body advises and consents. But in today's world, senators are particularly concerned that something dreadful about a nominee—damaging personal information especially—will not be uncovered until later and that they, the members of the committee, will be held accountable for carelessness. Thus, most nominees are closely scrutinized.

I was no exception. This was not only a cabinet-rank post but the OMB directorship is viewed by most authorities as one of the most powerful positions in government. Also, the committee I was going before was the same committee that had reviewed the qualifications of President Carter's first nominee to head OMB—Bert Lance.[5] So here comes another portly fellow who grew up in Georgia

---

[5] Lance, an old personal friend of President Carter's, easily won confirmation. However, subsequent questions about his dealings as a banker in Calhoun, Georgia, eventually forced his resignation. Many pundits blamed the Senate committee for not being sufficiently careful in its review of Lance's qualifications.

who wants to be OMB director; understandably, their review of my qualifications was intense, although I must say professional in every way.

Despite the relative ease with which I was confirmed, the experience brought home to me how much reform is needed in the confirmation process, which works in a way that is practically inexplicable to a neophyte to Washington. No doubt partly by design, it is tortuous for the nominee; members of Congress want the nominee to know that they are people to be reckoned with, and putting the nominee though an uncertain and often traumatic confirmation process serves that purpose. But the excesses of the process, I believe, are particularly harmful to government. On the whole, they tend to dampen the spirits of highly motivated nominees, shake their self-confidence, and, probably most important, cause many nominees to view Congress as the enemy once they are in office.

The Senate shows great deference to the prerogatives of colleagues. Thus, for example, when any member of a confirmation committee wishes to review a nominee's background more intensely or discuss with a nominee her or his particular concerns, the other members of the committee would not think of calling for a vote until each member was ready. Accordingly, frequently a confirmation hearing will be held and perhaps even a *markup* (a vote by the committee on the nominee) will be scheduled, only to be postponed at the last minute when some senator insists that he or she wishes to explore something further with the nominee. In some of those discussions, the senator seeks to extract promises from the nominee; in other situations, the senator is merely firing a shot across the nominee's bow.

Even after a nominee is approved by the relevant committee, a senator may place a hold on the nominee, temporarily preventing the full Senate from voting on the nominee's qualifications. All this creates uncertainty and sometimes economic hardship for the nominee. As a result, the nominee, once in office, tends to remember not the affirmative votes of the vast majority of senators but that she or he was "jerked around" by a few senators. The nominee may thus tend to blame the entire Senate membership, and maybe even members of the House of Representatives, for a very unpleasant process.

Hearing and confirmation

My hearing for the OMB directorship, held on September 24, 1985, was a big affair for my family. My mother-in-law flew in, as did my parents. I was introduced to the committee by my old friend and colleague Senator Phil Gramm (R., Tex.), who gave an extraordinary rendition of my background and endorsement of my nomination. I was glad my parents were there to hear what he said!

The remainder of the hearing went without any serious problems. Many questions were easily predicted: For example, "How will you balance the budget without raising taxes? Will you promise to come and testify at the committee's invitation? Will you give attention to the management responsibilities of OMB as well as its budget responsibilities?" Other questions were not so predictable. For example, "Why did the FTC urge the president not to grant import relief for domestic shoe producers? Why haven't you written anything on military preparedness?"

I was fairly certain one particular item would come up, and I was ready for it. In 1981, there was widespread criticism that the administration was cutting back on many programs to help the poor. At one point, in giving local school boards maximum flexibility to determine how to structure their school lunch programs, the Department of Agriculture proposed a rule clarifying nutrition requirements. One minor portion of that rule noted that condiments, such as relish or ketchup, might be considered as meeting the nutritional requirements of a vegetable. This regulation, apparently much delayed in being produced by the department, had been proffered to me at OMB for my approval. In a letter dated September 1, 1981, the department transmitted the regulation, noting that it was to be published in the *Federal Register* on September 4. According to records that I handed to the committee staff, I received and acknowledged receipt of same on September 4, the very day it appeared in the *Register*.

After the proposed rule was published, the administration's critics went crazy; "ketchup is a vegetable" became a rallying cry, and the story made the papers for many days in a row. Although troubled by the department's not following required procedures (specifically, they were required to send proposed rules over for clearance far in advance), when asked, I stated that, frankly, the rule had been misrepresented and, in fact, had much to commend it. (My concern was getting the most nutrition for kids out of a given lunch program budget.) Finally, however, on September 25, the president had had enough of the matter and announced to a group of reporters that he was ordering the "ketchup as a vegetable" rule withdrawn. I had the unenviable task of conveying that decision to the relevant officials at the department.

Thus, when Senator Eagleton (D., Mo.) asked me to comment on a press story that dredged up this episode two days before my confirmation hearing, I was ready with the relevant information. But I must confess to a certain disappointment; only the reporter who wrote the original story bothered to report my response, though many other reporters had made an issue of it. And whereas the day before my confirmation hearing the author of the original story stated as fact that I had been the administration official who approved the "ketchup is a vegetable" rule, the day of my hearing she simply reported that I denied I was the official who approved the rule.

This, I find, is a common trait among some reporters, who will report something as fact but, when faced with evidence to the contrary, will simply report that the one accused has denied the charge. I felt that fairness dictated that the news organization confess its error, but, alas, almost never do people in the media admit mistakes.

The hearing lasted only one day and was over by 2:30 P.M. Two days later the committee voted out my nomination unanimously, and then it went on the executive calendar of the Senate.

Technically, the Senate could have approved my nomination on Friday, September 27. It did not because Senate minority leader Robert Byrd (D., W. Va.) had been in a running battle with President Reagan over what are termed *recess appointments*. Under the Constitution, the president has the power to fill offices that are vacant during a congressional recess. In Byrd's view, Reagan had abused this privilege, and he demanded that Reagan not make any more recess appointments. For obvious reasons, the president was not about to abdicate any authority granted to him in the Constitution. Thus, there was a stalemate, during which some eight thousand appointments and promotions in the military were stalled, as well as approximately eighty presidential nominees (including judges), even though they had been approved by the committees of jurisdiction.

Days passed, during which my confirmation might have happened at any moment. But owing to the impasse over recess appointments and a few other glitches, it was not until October 4 that I was confirmed by a vote of ninety to two, with Vice-President Bush presiding. The next day, several of my colleagues from the FTC and I moved into our respective offices in the Old Executive Office Building. By Sunday, October 6, we were very much involved in matters at hand, including Senate action on the Gramm amendment to the national debt limit—a bill that would force the president and Congress to narrow the budget deficit to zero over a five-year period.

3 | **Welcome to OMB!**

As I walked into my new office at OMB on Saturday, October 5, I recalled a comment by one of my colleagues: a dog entering a new room marks all four corners, which meant I should at least rearrange the furniture. Although some of my staff had rearranged the furniture before I got there, after making some measurements, walking around the room, and thinking about it, I hit on a configuration that proved satisfactory over the next three years. (Taking time to make a new office arrangement attractive and functional is well worth the effort.) During the afternoon, boxes of books and paraphernalia arrived from the FTC. By evening, things were largely in their place, and I had even been able to read a few memos.

More important, around 11:00 in the morning, I asked Deputy Director Joe Wright to swear me in. In attendance were Mark Sullivan, Jeff Eisenach, Tim Muris, and a few others.

In true OMB style, I arrived for work early Sunday morning, forgoing Sunday morning church service. We had a lot ahead of us. I had concluded (see the next section) that the deficit must be the first priority and that to solve this problem required institutional change—a reform in the budget process to counterbalance the tendency of the federal government to rely on borrowing as a means of financing current spending. After all, in only one year out of the past twenty-five had the federal government balanced its budget. The propensity to engage in deficit finance, endemic to existing institutions, had to be changed.

Having solved the deficit problem the first year, I would then turn to the organization of the executive branch. As countless experts have concluded over the years, the current arrangement is a hodgepodge reflecting a history of Band-Aid approaches to public policy (a new issue emerging? no problem, establish a new agency). I found that lines of authority and responsibility were unclear; that formulation, coordination, and execution of policies were grossly inefficient; and that communications from the top down were practically nonexistent. Although this disarray made OMB a more powerful agency (being the only instrument capable of operationally managing the policy process), this was certainly no way to organize an efficient government.

As I was to find out, however, senior administration officials had little interest in reorganizing government—reflecting, perhaps, an unwillingness to address any proposal that might mean their giving up turf or to incur the wrath of congressional committees who might see their power and influence diminished.[1] More important, as should be abundantly clear, the deficit problem was not solved the first year. In a sense, all three years of my tenure at OMB were spent trying to resolve the budget problem, which left little opportunity for fundamental reform of government organization.[2]

Top priority: Reduce the deficit

Even though a major theme of then Governor Reagan's 1980 campaign had been to balance the budget, the deficit had ballooned enormously. For the fiscal year 1985 the deficit had set a record—$212.3 billion (up from $73.8 billion in 1980)—and appeared to be heading higher for the next fiscal year (it turned out to be $221.2 billion for fiscal year 1986; see figure 1).[3] Something had to be

---

[1] Attempts to reform government are much more likely to be successful if begun at the very beginning of an administration—before key appointees have become possessive of their agencies and while there is still something of a honeymoon with Congress. The regulatory review program I helped put in place in 1981 is an example: had the president not signed Executive Order 21866 during the first month of his term, the regulatory relief initiative probably never would have come about because of agency opposition to the new requirement of having OMB clear their regulatory proposals.

[2] I should not leave the impression that OMB's management activities during my tenure were limited to government reorganization. In fact, they built on earlier efforts of Dave Stockman, Ed Harper, and Joe Wright, were wide ranging (productivity improvement goals for government agencies, reduction of government waste, clarification of agency missions, privatization of government programs, and improvements in regulatory decision making, for example), and on the whole were quite successful. But I continue to believe that enormous taxpayer savings and improvements in service delivery could be realized by a thoroughgoing reorganization of the federal government.

[3] As explained in the Appendix, usually in January or February the president submits to Congress his recommended budget for the coming fiscal year—that is, for the fiscal year beginning the following October. In October 1985, the 1985 fiscal year had just ended and the 1986 fiscal year had just begun. Unless noted otherwise, reference to budgets will be in *fiscal* years, not calendar years. (For example, the 1987 budget covers the period October 1, 1986, through September 30, 1987.)

Figure I: Federal Deficits, 1980–1986

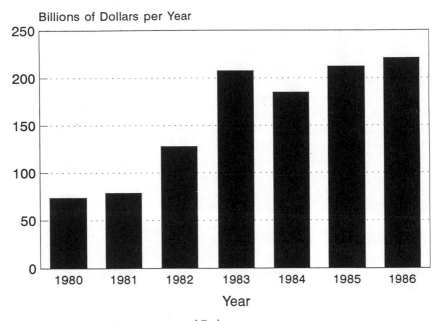

Source: Office of Management and Budget

done. But consistent with President Reagan's preferences and my own predilections, I thought this should be done by controlling spending, not by raising taxes.

Just how does one make Congress and the president reduce the deficit, much less do it by controlling spending? As the literature on public choice economics had amply demonstrated, elected representatives are unlikely to end their reliance on deficit finance or to control their impulses to spend at ever-increasing rates under the current institutional arrangements. The decision-making rules had to change to make it more painful for members of Congress and the president to finance government by means of debt and to engage in excessive spending.

Senator Phil Gramm had designed just such a proposal with the backing of two Senate powerhouses: Warren Rudman (R., N. H.) and Fritz Hollings (D., S. C.). Phil had discussed his plan with me before my confirmation, and I had encouraged Don Regan and OMB acting director Joe Wright to urge the president to support it. Such support was publicly announced on October 4, the day I was confirmed.

Phil's plan was directed at getting the deficit down in an orderly fashion rather than eliminating it overnight—something I had stressed as being the appropriate policy at my confirmation hearing. In the event Congress and the president didn't achieve the lower deficit target for the coming year, a last-resort "robot" mechanism would take over and cut spending across the board. The proposal was crude, had some procedural frailties, and was open to endless, crippling amendments. But it was brilliant, was the only game in town, and just might work. I decided to make deficit reduction my first priority and Gramm's amendment the means of achieving it.

Senate debate began on what would become Gramm-Rudman-Hollings on Sunday, my second day on the job. As a show of my personal interest, as well as administration support, I traveled to Capitol Hill to meet with Senators Gramm, Rudman, and Hollings in the vice-president's ceremonial office off the Senate floor. Senator Hollings was the last to join the meeting. Because we had been on opposite sides of the fence on a number of FTC issues, I leapt to my feet, grabbed his hand, and assured him that despite past differences we were on the same side on this issue and that with any luck we'd prevail. He seemed pleasant and mentioned that, when asked about me on a network television interview program, he had been supportive. For reasons of fairness, and also to increase the measure's bipartisan appeal, from then on I insisted that the measure be referred to as the Gramm-Rudman-*Hollings* bill, rather than the more frequently used Gramm-Rudman.[4]

Getting started

On Monday, October 7, the first normal working day, I drove myself to the office rather than being picked up by my new White House driver. For convenience, I followed Dave Stockman's convention, subsequently adopted by Joe Wright: begin the day with a 7:30 meeting of OMB senior staff, then on to the 8:00 get-together in the West Wing of the White House, which Jim Baker had called the *senior staff meeting* and which Don Regan later renamed the *White House operations meeting*.

My first reaction to the White House operations meetings was that they were too often driven by the news of the day. Don Regan would call on someone to summarize the president's schedule and then on Larry Speakes to discuss the day's major news stories. Although the president and his staff need to be responsive to the press and thus need an accurate reporting of what is going on, the questions too often were "What's happening today?" rather than "What should we be trying

---

[4] In ensuing months and years, I often corrected draft presidential speeches and releases to this effect.

to accomplish in the remainder of the president's term, and how should we get it done?"

My formal swearing in took place Tuesday, October 8, and it was a big day for the Miller clan. Just after noon, President Reagan welcomed my wife, Demaris, our kids, my mother and father, my mother-in-law, and me into the Oval Office. Also present were the vice-president and Don Regan. We shook hands all around and chatted briefly, during which time the president indicated his strong desire that I be tough on the budget; I responded that I surely would be. We then walked across to the Roosevelt Room amid a cornucopia of flashing lights, whirring cameras, and live microphones.

As we stood at our appointed places, President Reagan walked to the lectern and said some nice things about me and his expectations for my efforts. I then stepped to the lectern and said that I felt greatly honored at his having chosen me and at the Senate's having confirmed me and that with God's help as well as the help of those people in the room I would not let him down. Then Vice-President Bush administered the oath of office.

After the ceremony, at the vice-president's suggestion, the president wrote a note in our family Bible. Champagne was then served, and my former colleague Boyden Gray proposed a toast. Then, I had to get the family back to my office and wait until the 1:15 sitting for lunch in the White House mess.

Later in the day, there was a large reception in the courtyard of the New Executive Office Building involving much of the professional staff of OMB; I addressed the throng and introduced a number of the new people joining the staff.

Over the next few months I observed that one of the rewarding, and a little surprising, things was the ease with which the two staffs came together. OMB then had a director, a deputy director, and ten associate director–level positions. When I went over, six of those ten senior positions were open. Counting the deputy director, then, about half the senior staff knew the issues well but didn't know me well. Because I brought five of my FTC associates to fill five of the six vacancies, approximately half the senior staff knew me well but didn't know the OMB issues well. More important, the two groups didn't know each other well.

Knowing how important it is to engender teamwork, I immediately set about to make sure everyone fit in, which meant spending a good deal of time with the incumbent senior staff, assuring them that their efforts were recognized and appreciated. But it also meant spending a lot of time with the FTC crowd, some of whom, like me, needed to learn more about the agency and its personnel. Everyone, however, appeared to recognize the importance of sensitivity to others. The FTC crowd bent over backward not to be seen as insiders by birthright; the incumbent crowd helped make it possible for the new crowd to get its feet on the ground. In short, both groups were made up of seasoned professionals.

Dealing with the career staff at OMB worked in some respects the same way.

Few high-level officials in Washington who have dealt with OMB would deny the common observation that OMB is the elite of the government's civilian corps. Competition for analyst and budget examiner positions at OMB is fierce. A camaraderie there sees employees through the extraordinary hours demanded of them during budget season and beyond.[5] From the beginning, therefore, I reinforced that view. As things developed, I was never sorry that I took pains to treat the staff professionally, and when there were occasional lapses (for example, insisting that something go my way without explaining the rationale or without asking for their views), I always regretted it.

As we all know, there are numerous deadbeats in the civil service corps; however, there are also pockets of extraordinary talent with a commitment to public service far beyond what the public has a right to expect, given the disparaging remarks often leveled at government employees. In this respect, it is probably good that there is a "Washington culture" so that those public employees who do excel can receive applause from their peers. Having a large number of public employees in one place tends to generate competition that results in these pockets of excellence. As for the deadbeats, I view that as a problem of how civil servants are managed, which, in turn, is a function of the incentives and discretion afforded senior managers and the degree to which we hold them accountable.

The fact is, we do not place good management at much of a premium in the U.S. government. Incentives are structured around "new initiatives," which demand more employees. A manager is doing well if the demand for his service grows and he can justify hiring more workers. More employees for an organization makes everyone happy because it increases the likelihood that individuals within an organization will be promoted—they are the ones with the expertise. Organizations that show progress by reducing excess demand or even in the extreme by working themselves out of a job receive little reward. I have often wondered how some of the stalwarts at the Civil Aeronautics Board, especially those who argued eloquently for deregulation, have fared since deregulation began in 1980. If there is justice in civil service, then surely they have reaped significant rewards.

As with many high-powered jobs, a new OMB director has to hit the ground running. The fourth day on the job I was asked to make a major presentation on Gramm-Rudman-Hollings and the budget situation at a cabinet breakfast without the president. All members of the cabinet spoke highly of making severe cuts in spending to get within the president's goal of bringing the deficit down to 4, then 3, then 2 percent of the gross national product—a path consistent with the Gramm-Rudman-Hollings targets, should they be enacted. All during the meeting, I reflected that, almost without exception, each of these cabinet members

---

[5] Similar crunches occur for those involved in management, privatization, and regulatory issues.

had proposed budgets for 1987 in excess of earlier OMB guidance—which, even had it been followed, would have resulted in a deficit some $15 billion over the initial Gramm-Rudman-Hollings target.

In future conversations with cabinet members the expected emerged: everyone thought the budget should be cut, but almost everyone was convinced that their situation was unique—they needed more money, not less. It reminded me of the visits I had made to Capitol Hill before confirmation. Several senators had pressed on me the extraordinary seriousness of my position and the immense challenge of eliminating the budget deficit by controlling spending—a challenge I must not fail to meet. Then, just before I left, they stressed to me the need for a piece of pork[6] they simply must have funded, usually mentioning that my predecessor had "promised it" to them.

Thus, I realized that I would forever be called on by cabinet officers and members of Congress to say yes to their special programs. To do my job, I would have to say no far more frequently than yes. But I resolved always to say no with a smile on my face and a cordial tone in my voice.[7]

Developing the new budget

At the beginning of my third week at OMB, Don Regan, Joe Wright, and I met to discuss ways in which the fiscal year 1987 budget might be configured to meet the Gramm-Rudman-Hollings deficit target of $144 billion.[8] At first blush, this would not seem too difficult, for back around the first of August the Congressional Budget Office (CBO) had estimated the current services deficit for 1987 to be only (!) $155 billion. But we knew better. First, the economic assumptions on which these projections had been made were altogether too optimistic. Economic growth would likely be less than they had projected, thus lowering government revenues significantly and raising outlays, both effects increasing the projected

---

[6] *Pork* is defined as spending on projects that are of low priority for the nation as a whole but of high priority to the congressperson or senator who is "bringing home the bacon," helping ensure her or his reelection. Examples include many infrastructure projects ("highways to nowhere") and special grants to institutions of higher learning (more on this in chapter 8).

[7] At least that was my resolution. But like many resolutions . . .

[8] As this was November 1985, we were working on the budget for fiscal year 1987, which would begin on October 1, 1986.

[9] The current services budget extrapolates current law as if budget revenues and outlays were placed on automatic pilot (see the brief discussion in the Appendix and the longer discussion in chapter 10).

deficit. Moreover, the savings Congress claimed for its catchall reconciliation bill[10] appeared not to be coming about, and the appropriations committees seemed intent on approving several budget-busting bills that went far beyond spending limits in the budget resolution—that is, guidance Congress had set for itself and on which the CBO estimates had been predicated. Finally, owing to unusually good crop harvests, the costs of the farm program—pegged at $34.8 billion in the budget resolution—looked more like $50 billion. I remarked that only government could so screw up things that when harvests were good, taxpayers suffered.[11]

Instead of facing a 1987 deficit of $155 billion, we were, in fact, facing prospects of a budget deficit exceeding the previous year's record of $212.3 billion. (The budget deficit proved to be a record $221 billion in 1986.) Thus, in this and subsequent meetings, we decided it absolutely necessary to hold the line on outlays and to urge the president to adopt a veto strategy to police excessive spending. This would apply not only to appropriations measures and existing entitlement programs but also to the new farm bill—a budget-buster in the making. We also agreed to urge the president to oppose any tax increase because any forthcoming revenues would likely be used not to reduce the deficit but to fund new spending.

Each Monday, except when he was away from Washington, President Reagan lunched with Vice-President Bush and several members of the White House senior staff, usually in the cabinet room. This was called the President's Monday issues luncheon. Soon after our meetings on the budget, I made a presentation to the president and the senior staff at one of these Monday luncheons. This was my first substantive face-to-face meeting with the president on the budget (literally so, since the vice-president was out of town and I was sitting in his seat, directly across from the president). I briefly discussed the Gramm-Rudman-Hollings situation on the Hill and the difficulties we expected to encounter in meeting those deficit targets because of deteriorating economic circumstances and a lack of congressional will and urged a veto strategy to force Congress to keep within the spending targets set in the budget resolution.[12] His response was direct and

[10] As described in the Appendix, the reconciliation bill contains changes in tax laws and changes in laws affecting spending on permanent programs such as Social Security and Medicare—entitlement programs.

[11] Greater harvests increase budget outlays and thus harm taxpayers in two ways. First, there is more production on which to pay a subsidy. Second, larger sales depress prices, which widens the per unit subsidy (that is, the difference between the target price and the market price).

[12] Even though we were well into the 1986 budget year, Congress had not passed all the budget laws; instead, discretionary appropriations had been facilitated by a temporary law called a *continuing resolution* (see the Appendix).

specific: we would meet the Gramm-Rudman-Hollings targets in the new budget whether or not they were codified into law, and he would freely wield the veto pen if appropriations measures were passed exceeding the budget resolution for 1986.[13] This reinforced our resolve and made our task a lot easier.

The president had said earlier that in coming up with a 1987 budget we could not touch Social Security, we had to assure a 3 percent real growth in defense, and we could not propose any new tax measures. (Nor, of course, could we do much about interest expense, except to get the deficit down and hope for lower interest rates.) This left less than half the budget—just over $430 billion— from which we had to achieve some $50 billion in savings from the spending level most had expected (that is, current services).

So, we began to battle on two fronts: keeping 1986 spending under control and finding places to cut budget requests for 1987. We also had to get Gramm-Rudman-Hollings passed in a form acceptable to the president.

---

[13] Any increases for 1986 would raise the spending baseline and make it more difficult to meet the deficit target for 1987.

4 | Gramm-Rudman-Hollings and the Debt Ceiling Crisis

THE OVERARCHING FEATURE of the Reagan administration's strategy to reduce the deficit and control spending in late 1985 was to enact Gramm-Rudman-Hollings. This was to prove difficult, not because Congress was reluctant to pass deficit-reduction legislation but because it was eager to pass it in a form the president would find unacceptable.

Enacting Gramm-Rudman-Hollings

The original (Gramm) form of the Gramm-Rudman-Hollings law was fairly clean and flexible. Everything except Social Security would be subject to across-the-board cuts or sequestration if the estimated deficit exceeded the target.[1] Also, in the event of a sequester, the adverse impact on the defense program could be minimized by reducing (within limits) the cuts in defense and by assuring sufficient flexibility within defense accounts so that the president could trade off one weapons system against another (in order to secure the strongest defense for any given [smaller] level of expenditure). As the legislative process proceeded, however, amendment after amendment sought clarification of the way sequestration

---

[1] As explained in the Appendix, budget authority is analogous to money in your checkbook, whereas budget outlays are the checks you write. If it appeared that outlays would exceed expected revenues by more than the deficit target, the president would be empowered to reduce budget authority in every budget account except Social Security by an amount sufficient to force outlays, and then the deficit, down to the target level(s).

would work, and, in nearly every case, the effect was to make the law, in the president's eyes, a less attractive mechanism.

Also, in the original version, Gramm-Rudman-Hollings would have sequestered defense spending in proportion to its share of the spending base—that is, total spending minus interest expense and Social Security. This would have led to defense's bearing only 43 percent of any outlay reduction under a sequester. Given the sentiment of Congress, however, it was not surprising to see the conferees gravitating toward a 50-50 rule: if any cuts were mandated, half would come from defense, half from nondefense accounts. Even in the original version of the bill, a sequester would have fallen inordinately hard on defense because to reduce defense spending by one dollar, defense budget authority must be cut by approximately two dollars.[2] Thus, the president (not to mention Cap Weinberger and the Joint Chiefs of Staff!) was troubled by the evolution of the Gramm-Rudman-Hollings amendment. Nothing we were able to do—cajoling, promising to be flexible on other bills, and so forth—would turn Congress from going this direction.

Legislative amendments then began taking away from the president any flexibility he might have had to distribute the cuts under a sequester. For one thing, the congressional leaders' priorities were different from those of President Reagan, and they feared he might use any flexibility to gut those programs he had previously proposed terminating but which Congress repeatedly had refused to cut. For another, members of Congress were protective of their own special-interest programs. So, if any programs were to be sequestered, these would bear no more than a proportional cut. Finally, the major, but seldom discussed, rationale was to tie the president's hands even further on defense, making the bill even less palatable to him.[3]

Then the Democratic leadership began exempting a variety of sensitive programs from the sequester, making it less objectionable from their standpoint. In addition to Social Security, low-income maintenance programs were made

---

[2] Again, as just noted, budget authority is the commitment for spending, whereas budget outlays are actual spending. (Budget authority is analogous to money put into a bank account, whereas budget outlays are analogous to writing and clearing checks.) In slow-spending accounts like defense, budget authority appropriated in any given year is frequently more important than how much is actually spent. To reduce spending a given amount, budget authority has to be reduced much more because a large portion of the year's spending will be from budget authority appropriated in previous years.

[3] When faced with the prospect that a sequester could lead to the discharge of troops—disbanding whole divisions—Congress gave the president authority to exempt the military personnel account but required the shortfall to be taken out of other defense accounts (primarily procurement).

fully exempt, and various other programs, including Medicare and veterans' benefits, were made partially exempt. In the end, the domestic programs fully liable for sequester totaled less than spending on defense.[4]

In retrospect, it appears that the Reagan administration and Congress were pursuing a Gramm-Rudman-Hollings strategy but with different goals in mind. Although both sides couched their rhetoric in terms of a need to reduce the deficit, the administration saw the law as a device to accomplish two ends: (1) commit Congress to firm, but realistic, targets for gradually eliminating the deficit over a period of five years and (2) force Congress to meet those goals by cutting spending, not by raising taxes. The mere threat of the automatic sequester (the "club in the closet") would make Congress meet the targets voluntarily, and, after all the ballyhoo over achieving a breakthrough on the deficit, Congress wouldn't change the targets. (We proved to be wrong on both accounts.) With the president's presumed ability to sustain a veto over any tax increase, we saw Congress acquiescing to budget cuts rather than our having to accept any tax increases. (In the end, we proved to be wrong on this as well.)

To put it bluntly, the majority of the members of Congress saw Gramm-Rudman-Hollings as a means to force the president to finally come to terms with the deficit by raising taxes. In retrospect, their perspective appears rational, and surely they set about with dispatch to modify the proposal to suit this objective. As just described, they endeavored to increase the hit on defense from any sequester. Moreover, they exempted most social programs from a potential sequester. Many, if not most, in Congress held out hope that the final version of Gramm-Rudman-Hollings would be so unpalatable to President Reagan that he would veto it, and thereby Congress, and surely the Democrats, would finally have gotten the upper hand on the deficit issue.[5] This, in turn, might well lead to a congressional solution—that is, an increase in taxes.

Should this strategy fail, most members of Congress thought the mere specter of a substantial hit on defense would bring the president to his senses. In fact, during the 1987 budget cycle immediately following the passage of Gramm-Rudman-Hollings, I was often approached by members of the congressional Democratic leadership offering a deal, usually of the following form: if we'd agree

---

[4] Also, under the heavily amended version of Gramm-Rudman-Hollings, for some members of Congress a sequester might even have been welcomed: it would hit defense, it would get the deficit down, but it would not touch sacred cow domestic programs. Such members were a distinct minority, however.

[5] Opinion polls continue to show that the public blamed Congress more for the deficit than it did the president. That view persists. See, for example, "Federal Spending, Taxes, and the Budget Deficit," a report conducted by the Roper Organization for Citizens for a Sound Economy Foundation (January 25, 1989).

to raise taxes by $20 billion, $10 billion would go to defense and $10 billion would go to domestic programs. I said no to all such entreaties, noting that for us the deal had two bads (increased domestic spending and increased taxes) and only one good (increased defense spending). Moreover, I had no doubt that as soon as I showed any interest in such a deal, word would leak that President Reagan had changed his mind on taxes.

In this context, it is not surprising that the administration was unsuccessful in restraining Congress from amending the original version of Gramm-Rudman-Hollings—the version the president endorsed the day I was confirmed as OMB director.[6] The fact was, Congress had him over a barrel. He could hardly forswear the goal of deficit reduction, which he would be perceived as doing if he vetoed the bill. But neither could he countenance a sequester that threatened his defense buildup. After all, he had staked enormous political capital on the proposition that, when the Soviets concluded they couldn't win the cold war, they'd come to the bargaining table.

To make matters worse, the Democrats in the House began chastising the Senate Republicans for having passed Gramm-Rudman-Hollings in language that did not appear to be binding until 1987. Whereas the Senate version called for a $180 billion deficit target for 1986 (that is, the fiscal year just begun), House Democrats said that doing something about the budget deficit ought to hurt now and promptly passed a bill with a $162 billion deficit target that would be binding immediately.

This scared the hell out of the Pentagon. According to our internal forecasts, this would have meant an immediate sequester of something on the order of $30 billion, with half of this coming out of defense and with no flexibility within spending accounts. Also, for reasons mentioned earlier, the budget authority hit for defense would be at least twice the hit in outlays. Thus, under the Democrats' bill, the president would have been faced with either accepting as much as a 10 percent real reduction in defense appropriations for 1986 or going along with an immediate increase in taxes. When I told the president what the Democrat's bill meant, his face got red, and he said, "Well, they better not send it down here because I'll veto it!" He thus revealed the price he would not pay for a Gramm-Rudman-Hollings bill.

One problem in seeing Gramm-Rudman-Hollings through the legislative process was that the administration had little credibility on budget issues because everyone knew it was shilling for defense, and defense had few friends. Since 1981, the defense budget had risen 50 percent in real terms, whereas domestic

---

[6] The president protested to me numerous times: "This is not the version of Gramm-Rudman-Hollings that I endorsed!"

Figure 2:   Gramm-Rudman-Hollings Deficit Targets, 1986–1991

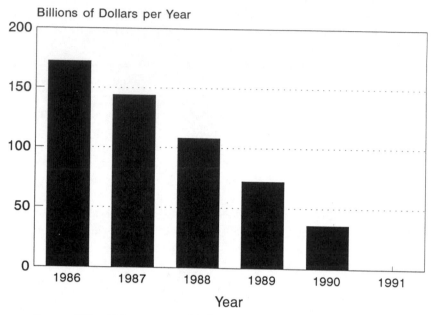

Billions of Dollars per Year

Year

SOURCE: Office of Management and Budget

discretionary spending in real terms was about the same as it had been in 1981.[7] Although everyone knows how difficult it is to close down obsolete military installations, politicians like handing out domestic pork more than military pork. It's the kind of pork that feeds more people and goes further politically. Thus, members of Congress had had their hands tied all this time so that defense might grow, and quite frankly they had had enough of it. To many on the Hill, the very idea of cutting domestic spending further without hitting defense many times over was laughable.

In the end, both sides won a victory of sorts, but, more important, the American people won. Gramm-Rudman-Hollings, which was signed into law on December 12, 1985, established declining deficit targets to a balanced budget in 1991 (see figure 2). More important, it provided a mechanism to force Congress and the president to meet those targets.

Despite strong efforts by Republicans and defense-minded Democrats on

---

[7] In real terms, entitlement spending had continued to rise.

Capitol Hill, the congressional leadership prevailed on the overall Gramm-Rudman-Hollings sequester formula: half from defense and half from domestic programs, with most social programs exempted. But the president prevailed in keeping the formula based on spending, not taxes. That is, if there were to be an automatic program to reduce the deficit, it would do its work on the spending side, not the revenue side. This, arguably, gave the president leverage because he was in favor of smaller government, whereas the congressional leadership was in favor of larger government. However, as we shall see, the threat of a sequester to defense was more than enough to balance the scales.

The American people won because whereas the deficit had been creeping up ominously, the year after enactment the deficit fell dramatically (from $221 billion in 1986 to $150 billion in 1987). But to some extent the victory was Pyrrhic: the Gramm-Rudman-Hollings sequester trigger mechanism was later to be held unconstitutional.[8]

The debt ceiling crisis

While we were shepherding Gramm-Rudman-Hollings through Congress, we were also drawn into a crisis created by Congress's refusal to increase the legal ceiling on the national debt.

For years, Congress's, acting in a thoroughly irresponsible way, has passed continuing resolutions and then allowed them to expire. That is, rather than passing thirteen individual appropriations measures before the end of the fiscal year as required under the 1974 Budget and Accounting Act, at the end of the fiscal year Congress would incorporate all remaining spending measures into a catchall continuing resolution. To avoid being a laughingstock, Congress would place a termination date in the continuing resolution to force itself to act. The only problem is that sometimes it didn't, or when it did, it would propose a continuing resolution that contained features unacceptable to the president.

Thus, approximately once a year the government would go into hibernation on the day the continuing resolution expired. All affected employees would report to work and go through the process of shutting down. At noon, all but essential employees would be sent home, with the rest going through the process of securing

---

[8] Under Gramm-Rudman-Hollings, a sequester would be ordered by the president, based upon a report by the director of CBO and the director of OMB, as amended by the comptroller general (that is, the head of the General Accounting Office). At issue was whether an employee of another branch of government could, in a sense, direct the president to do something. I repeatedly warned the bill's sponsors of the constitutional defect and urged them to remedy it—to no avail.

records for posterity. Of course, everyone knew it was all a joke, and the shutdown usually occurred in a festive mood. Within a few hours, Congress would come to its senses, pass a continuing resolution acceptable to the president, the president would sign it, and everything would get back to normal.

But in November 1985, we faced a different kind of shutdown. Almost by coincidence, we faced on November 15 not only the expiration of a continuing resolution but the national debt's coming up against the legal ceiling.

In a world of imperfect information and differences in priorities, elected officials frequently devise mechanisms that allow them to prove their support of one faction of constituents and also prove their support of just the opposite faction. The Occupational Safety and Health Act (OSHA) is a case in point. It contains admonishing language about the need to improve workers' health and safety and gives the OSHA agency considerable latitude in achieving this objective. Thus, on the one hand, a legislator can tell labor constituents how strong she or he has been in support of legislation that will protect them throughout their working lives. On the other hand, when the agency goes out and exercises this great discretion in a way many feel is required by the statute, the legislator can rail at "bureaucrats gone wild" before business groups and get a standing ovation.

Similarly, a legislator can, on the one hand, vote repeatedly for pet appropriations projects (pork in the eyes of some). The beneficiaries of this largesse are fairly cognizant of the benefits bestowed by the legislator (and if they are not, he will make sure they become so), whereas taxpayers in general are less knowledgeable about the burdens they bear. On the other hand, the same legislator gets to vote against an increase in the debt ceiling and can rail for hours against the "big spenders" and the "wastrels," to the delight of the fiscal conservatives he represents. In the end, however, the debt ceiling is always raised (see figure 3).[9] Many vote no, but a majority vote yes, explaining their action on the basis that they were forced into such an undesirable act, with the only alternative being bankruptcy for the nation.

In early October 1985, Treasury Secretary Jim Baker indicated to Congress that the U.S. government would run out of money around the first of November.[10] He urged quick action on the debt ceiling and, concomitantly, on Gramm-Rudman-Hollings because a substantial minority in the Senate refused to go along with an increase in the debt ceiling without responsible action on the

---

[9] The figure illustrates the debt ceiling as of the end of the fiscal year (see *Budget of the United States Government, Fiscal Year 1991*, p. A-305).

[10] It was not possible to give a definitive date because (a) it is difficult to predict revenues and outlays precisely, and (b) there exists a little give in the system because the Treasury Department typically runs positive balances, and these can be drawn down to some extent in an emergency.

Figure 3:   Federal Debt Limits, 1980–1985

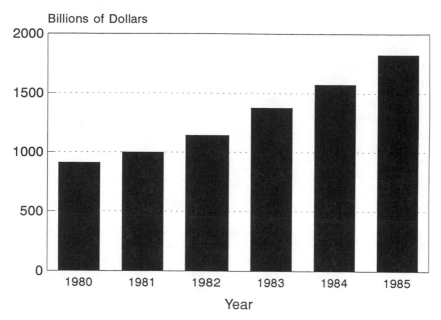

SOURCE: Office of Management and Budget

deficit.[11] On October 9, however, analysts at the Department of the Treasury concluded that it would be possible for the federal government to use some $15 billion in federal financing bank authority to, in effect, go above the debt ceiling. This hurt our credibility, for many on Capitol Hill began to believe that we were simply crying wolf and that, when the chips were down, we would find some other avenue for coming up with the money.

Toward the middle of November, however, all avenues were exhausted except the sale of gold at Fort Knox, which President Reagan adamantly opposed. Thus, a default on U.S. government securities—the first ever in two hundred years— seemed not only feasible but, to many high officials, likely. The results would have been tragic. First, the failure of the government to pay its financial obligations would mean that federal financial instruments would no longer be viewed as risk-free. Not only would we lose face internationally, but interest rates would go up, increasing the cost of debt service in our federal budget and raising interest

---

[11] Indeed, as mentioned earlier, the Gramm-Rudman-Hollings act originated as an amendment to the bill raising the debt ceiling.

costs all across the nation. Second, we would have to stop writing checks, and many who rightfully depended on the federal government—whether for welfare or simply receiving payment for goods or services rendered—would be hurt.

As a default appeared to be imminent, two related problems presented themselves. The first was to bring to the attention of those in Congress and the media that this was not simply another exercise in shutting down the government because of an expiration of appropriations. The consequences were far more serious. Second, there needed to be some contingency planning in the event a default did occur. Initially, I recommended to the president that he begin deferring payments on lower-priority programs around the first of November. Quick, draconian action at that time would have enabled the federal government to have gotten into December without having to default. [12] However, the president rejected this approach. Thus, our contingency planning focused on what to do should a default occur. Accordingly, my staff drew up an extensive memorandum, which I edited and reedited several times, directing each agency in the event of a default not to pay its bills—not to pay anything in any form whatsoever until further notice.

Understandably, we endeavored to get Congress's attention about this matter and to stir up general concern among the media and the public. On Friday, October 25, I appeared on the McLaughlin "One-on-One" show. On Sunday, October 27, I did "This Week with David Brinkley." On Friday, November 1, I addressed the National Press Club, which carried my address live on the Cable News Network. On the following Tuesday I did the "Today" show. I also did a presentation in the White House newsroom lambasting Congress for its inaction and stating the consequences of failing to raise the debt ceiling. Two days before the Treasury was expected to run out of money, Jim Baker and I addressed the White House press corps, emphasizing the gravity of the situation; I also distributed a copy of the memorandum (mentioned above) that I was sending to all agency heads instructing them in case of a default.

The result was that those who wanted to hold the big spenders' feet to the fire blinked first. That is, the congressional budget cutters gave in to the big spenders and agreed to an increase in the debt ceiling—without Gramm-Rudman-Hollings. To me, this illustrates how disingenuous the big spenders are with their protestations over the budget deficit and how willing they are to go to any lengths to avoid hits on their pet programs.

Being new to the job, and having to face the immediate needs of developing the 1987 budget, shepherding Gramm-Rudman-Hollings through Congress, and dealing with the debt ceiling crisis, I turned the matter of guiding final passage

---

[12] December's cash inflow from corporate income tax payments would have bought more time.

of the 1986 appropriations bills over to Joe Wright.[13] Here, we played something of a "good cop–bad cop" routine. Joe would discuss with the appropriations subcommittee chairmen our concerns with their bills. Many of them would claim that although their budget totals were over the limits imposed by the congressional budget resolution, they had an agreement with another subcommittee to provide *offsets* (spend less than the budget resolution allowed). But their stories didn't jibe. In some cases, subcommittee chairmen claimed that the Defense Department had agreed to deductions from its budget—for example, to fund operations of the U.S. Coast Guard.[14] Joe would take what appeared to be the most reasonable proposal and bring it to me. I would then express great disappointment and consternation, ending with some variant of the "millions for defense, but not one penny for blackmail" speech, and Joe would go back and report that I would accept the deal. But by hanging tough and rejecting all but the most reasonable proposals, we saved billions of dollars from the 1986 appropriations and kept the 1986 deficit from being any higher than it turned out to be—a record $221 billion.

Progressing on the 1987 budget, I went through all thirteen of the director's reviews and made major cuts in proposed spending. A week or so later, all these incremental budget decisions were compiled into a single new volume that showed we were still some $15 billion over the $144 billion Gramm-Rudman-Hollings deficit target. I returned the material to the OMB associate directors for a further ratcheting-down process. But contrary to previous practice, I did not want any simple macrosolution, such as across-the-board freezes or percentage reductions. Instead, I directed that calls be made on the merits of the programs and that the merits should consist of the analytic merits, not the political feasibility.

During this period of internal deliberation over the 1987 budget, we were faced with agencies' repeated attempts to circumvent the process. Despite an executive-branch prohibition on discussing the president's budget before it is submitted to Congress (a rule going back to at least President Truman), every year public officials jump the gun to secure funding of their pet programs. The fall of 1985 was no exception. For example, when money for the U.S. Coast Guard appeared threatened, the Coast Guard commandant ordered a major portion of its flotilla to stay in port and announced that the agency would no longer be able to support the president's drug interdiction program. (I was given

---

[13] At the time, most appropriated programs had been extended by means of a continuing resolution (see the Appendix).

[14] We discovered that some of these stories relative to defense were true. I called both Cap Weinberger and Deputy Defense Secretary Will Taft to complain because it hurt our credibility in arguing against cuts in defense. As it turned out, they had no knowledge of what their subordinates had been up to and put a stop to it.

to understand that this is their version of the Washington Monument Game[15] and that it occurs once a year right on schedule.) A cabinet officer announced a new safety program he said would be included in the 1987 budget. Some of the military people started making presentations on the Hill about how they were going to spend funds in 1987. In each case, I took swift action to let those officials know they were violating the president's rules. However, the hemorrhaging became so great that I ended up sending out a memorandum to the head of each agency reminding them of the president's prerogatives and instructing them not to compromise the president's flexibility by announcing anything related to the 1987 budget.

In late November, I met with Richard Wirthlin to discuss possible themes for the 1987 budget. He pointed out the importance of highlighting a few simple ideas to maximize communication with the public at large. In this respect, his views were absolutely coincident with mine; I had long been convinced that the only way to market a major budget realignment was to talk in terms of principles and themes. It is virtually impossible to win if you take on the budget issue by issue. Every program has its constituency, and every constituency hires its own analysts to prove that this program, perhaps above all others, deserves to be funded. The further down the budget you go in terms of detail, the fewer opportunities there are for orchestrating social compacts wherein each participant gives up something to accomplish more in the end.

Of particular interest to me in the discussion with Wirthlin was his conclusion that if we were trying to maximize the defense budget for 1987, the best way was to take some cuts off the top to show reasonableness and then hold fast at the lower figure. In the end, this is the strategy the president chose to employ.

On December 3, the president met with the GOP leadership[16] and asked me to speak on Gramm-Rudman-Hollings. I made a strong pitch for the bill but in a form that would reduce to a minimum the sequester for 1986 and allow sufficient flexibility among defense accounts. The leaders were sympathetic but responded that they didn't have enough votes to affect the outcome. The president was nonplussed about the lack of prospects for an acceptable bill.

---

[15] The Washington Monument Game refers to an apocryphal story wherein the president assembles his cabinet, tells them their spending plans are over budget, and orders them to review their budgets to establish priorities so they will know where to cut. The next week the cabinet reassembles, and the secretary of the interior reports that after thorough review he's identified the lowest priority: he proposes closing the Washington Monument. This tactic, of course, is designed to assure full funding of his budget, as what president wants to be responsible for closing the Washington Monument?

[16] These meetings were held in the cabinet room with twenty or so Republican congressional leaders; the bipartisan leadership meetings were similar affairs, but with the number of leaders limited to approximately ten from each party.

Of particular concern was the possible adverse effects on the defense budget. The sequester, if there was one, could hit defense hard.

Three days later, Deputy Secretary of Defense Will Taft and the Joint Chiefs of Staff met with the president to express their serious misgivings about Gramm-Rudman-Hollings. The show these gentlemen put on was extraordinary. To begin with, they had charts that I estimated to be four feet high and eight feet long—the size of a sheet of plywood. It took two easels to hold them and a man at each end to change them. My thought was, "Only the Defense Department can afford charts like these!"

Despite the fact that defense spending had grown 50 percent in real terms during the Reagan presidency, from the presentation you would have thought the department was at its last gasp and that Gramm-Rudman-Hollings would finish off the job. I've never seen the Washington Monument Game played to such extremes. All the president's favorite programs were conjured up as being threatened by Gramm-Rudman-Hollings. The total amount of the threats was conjured up as being in the neighborhood of a quarter of the defense budget—not the 2 or 3 percent threatened by Gramm-Rudman-Hollings in 1986.[17]

Each defense service chief made his pitch. The army chief said that his men would have virtually no tanks to protect them. The marine chief said that 14 percent of his personnel would have to be discharged. The navy chief said that portions of the fleet would have to be mothballed. The air force chief said that principal weapons systems would have to be curtailed. And they all agreed that this would mean the end of the volunteer army.[18]

At the conclusion of the presentation, the president expressed appreciation for the military's dilemma. But he also presented the chiefs with a few facts of life. He noted that during the 1980 campaign he had often been asked what he would do if the chips were down and he had to choose between running a deficit and strengthening defense. He always answered strengthen defense, which would get a round of applause. But today, said the president, when he made such statements, there was dead silence—a fact that he attributed both to the national defense having been strengthened considerably and to what he viewed as unconscionable misrepresentations of alleged excesses (coffee pots, toilet seats, hammers, and the like).

So, the chiefs had their say, their opportunity to make their pitch, and they

---

[17] The current version of Gramm-Rudman-Hollings, reflecting a compromise with the Senate, did not envision so great a sequester for 1986 as did the original House version mentioned earlier.

[18] I suspected they made this argument partly for my benefit as I have been a longtime supporter of the volunteer army. See, for example, James C. Miller III, ed., *Why the Draft?: The Case for a Volunteer Army* (New York: Penguin Books, 1968).

went all out. But they also heard an important message, which was the difficulty of maintaining their accustomed buildup in the current political climate. My hopes began to rise that the president would find Gramm-Rudman-Hollings acceptable after all.

The president and the 1987 budget

Right after the Joint Chiefs made their opposition to Gramm-Rudman-Hollings clear, Joe Wright, Tim Muris, Al Keel, and I briefed the president and the White House senior staff on the budget we'd been preparing, taking care to collect all the notebooks after the meeting (except the president's) to "protect the innocent" should there be leaks. My strategy was to show the president that he had had remarkable success in meeting those objectives he had set forth in his 1980 campaign except one. The opening part of the presentation indicated, with graphs, the progress that had been made in strengthening national defense, lowering the inflation rate, raising domestic incomes, reducing tax rates, and so forth. The last chart was of the budget deficit, and here there was not progress but regress. Thus, I told the president, the challenge of the 1987 budget is to turn the situation around with respect to the deficit without endangering the progress made in securing these other objectives.

I next broke down the budget into component parts, pointing out that I was observing his admonitions: (a) no new taxes, (b) no tampering with Social Security, and (c) a 3 percent real increase for defense. The first chart (partly reproduced in figure 4) showed our projections of total spending (1986 through 1989) reflecting the following components: interest on the national debt, Social Security, defense, and all other, which would be the source of the necessary savings. I then broke down the all other component into three major subcomponents: low-income maintenance, medical and retirement benefits, and domestic discretionary programs (see figure 5).

I suggested that the appropriate approach would be to take very little from the national debt,[19] none from Social Security, none from defense (in fact increase it), and adjust the last component as necessary to meet the Gramm-Rudman-Hollings deficit target. Because we were estimating the budget deficit to be on the order of $194 billion for 1987 based on an extrapolation of current receipts and current spending, we had to cut about $50 billion from the current services baseline of some $430 billion; within this component we should go after princi-

---

[19] By reducing the deficit we would reduce interest expense for two reasons: first, because there would be less debt to service and, second, because there would be a slight reduction in interest rates (less crowding out of domestic investment).

Figure 4: Baseline Projections of Total Spending

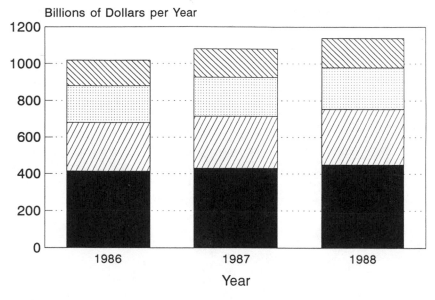

Billions of Dollars per Year

SOURCE: Office of Management and Budget

pally the third subcomponent, domestic discretionary programs. I then explained that my approach was to examine various programs and determine whether they were appropriately a federal function, given the president's political philosophy. If not, should they be transferred to state and local governments or to the private sector? For those programs that should remain in the federal sector, the next question was whether they were at their appropriate levels—should they be expanded, contracted, or even eliminated? Finally, for whatever programs remained, could they not be run more efficiently (that is, at lower cost)?[20]

I told the president that I would present the budget details the following Monday and that they would include program reductions asked for in previous budgets but not approved by Congress. But I also told him there were significant additional program reductions and some asset sales, which I described to him in the following way:

---

[20] This is a stylized version of the decision calculus. Of course, decisions over efficiency and the amount of spending are interrelated.

Figure 5: Sources of Savings, 1986–1988

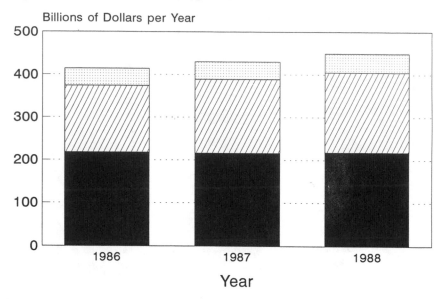

Billions of Dollars per Year

■ Other Programs ▨ Medical, Retirement ☐ Low Income Support

Source: Office of Management and Budget

> We have a lot of assets in the federal government, some of which we keep around mostly for nostalgic reasons. We're sort of like the family that is hard up for cash whose Aunt Nellie gave them her car when she died twenty years ago and it's been out in the shed ever since. Along comes some fellow and offers $6,000 for the old bucket and plans to restore it. Of course, the family doesn't want to give up Aunt Nellie's automobile, but it's better to do that than do without.

The president agreed.

I also pointed out to him that efforts to privatize many government activities are usually driven by analyses showing that such programs would be operated more efficiently in the private sector, primarily because the private sector's superior incentive structure leads to a more efficient allocation of resources. So, here we have asset sales being driven by both reasons—more efficient resource allocation and helping us through a difficult period of meeting Gramm-Rudman-Hollings deficit targets.[21] Moreover, I mentioned that in some areas—particularly

---

[21] According to our forecast, if Congress adopted the measures we advocated, the deficit path would almost coincide with the Gramm-Rudman-Hollings deficit target path for subsequent years. In a sense, then, the pain would have to be incurred only once.

financial portfolios—privatization would result in better decision making on the part of Congress because the real costs of subsidy and guarantee programs would be revealed when the decisions were made. I also stressed that the budget included other management improvements, and President Reagan seemed particularly interested in these. The president's overall response to this meeting was encouraging, for in addition to providing guidance, he revealed that my thinking about what he was looking for was largely correct.

The scheduled presentation to the president for the following Monday was postponed for two reasons. First, even though we worked mightily over the weekend, we were unable to have the materials fully checked and double-checked in time for the session. Second, we began to see leaks of information about the budget and speculation about what it would contain just as Congress was formulating the final version of Gramm-Rudman-Hollings. Obviously, we didn't want to upset the applecart with spurious stories about details of the president's budget. So we rescheduled the meeting for Wednesday. (The reschedule caused some problems because, in a meeting with the press the previous Friday afternoon, I had indicated that I would share with them some of the highlights of Monday's session with the president.)

In the meeting with the president on Wednesday, I began by reviewing the taxonomy of the budget described the previous week and showing what the proposed changes would do in each category. I then set forth the major issues— those areas in which I proposed major program reductions and those where we could expect controversy even though the changes were not particularly large. Each issue was illustrated with a graph containing a detailed description of the effects. I ended by showing the overall effects of these changes during the *out years* (the years following 1987). My purpose here was to stress that if we got spending under control in 1987, it would be reasonably easy to meet the Gramm-Rudman-Hollings targets in the subsequent four years and thus achieve a balanced budget in 1991.

On a number of issues the president raised questions, made decisions, and occasionally illustrated the point I was making with an anecdote. Overall, however, he endorsed the package and even pronounced it good. I realized, of course, that he had been through most of these issues before. But I was also gratified that in the new initiatives we were kindred spirits.

My fondest remembrance from that day relates to my presentation about the Interstate Commerce Commission:

> Mr. President, if the Interstate Commerce Commission ever had a public interest rationale, that evaporated with the proliferation of competition and the recent steps toward deregulation. Mr. President, in 1987 the Interstate Commerce Commission will be one hundred years old—it's the oldest of our regulatory agencies. And one hundred years of misguided regulation is long enough!

The president heartily concurred. But he also noted that there would be significant opposition to eliminating the agency, primarily from the trucking industry.

The following day, the president met with the cabinet and asked me to present the 1987 budget. In the past, rightly or wrongly, agency heads had taken an adversarial role with OMB over the budget, and consequently cabinet members often did not find out what OMB had in store for them until they sat down before the president. In my judgment, this adversarial relationship was also responsible, at least to some extent, for cabinet and other agency officials giving only lackluster support to the president's budget and even on occasion working behind the scenes on Capitol Hill to save programs in contradiction to the president's policies. I realized that for this budget to have any chance of enactment, we needed the strong support of all agency officials.

Thus, I set about trying to engender teamwork by insisting that all agency heads be called beforehand so that they knew what was coming. Specifically, I called all cabinet agency heads; Joe Wright called the heads of all major noncabinet agencies (such as the Environmental Protection Agency and the Veterans Administration); and the program associate directors called all the other agency heads. This small courtesy, I believe, paid sizable dividends, for I was told that cabinet officer responses to the budget were not nearly as adverse as in previous years and that there were fewer appeals of OMB budget decisions. Consequently, I concluded that cabinet support for the budget was likely to be far greater than it had been.

At the cabinet meeting, the president voiced his strong feelings about the need to reduce the deficit by reducing domestic spending—not by raising taxes or cutting into defense. He called on all the agencies to do their part and to work for the implementation of his budget on Capitol Hill. He then turned to me, saying, "Okay, Jim, now draw blood!" At that, I merely stared down at my book and after the laughter ceased said, "Mr. President, I suspect the first blood to be drawn will be from my own veins!" I then presented to the cabinet an abbreviated version of what I had presented to the president. The president reiterated that this budget had been reviewed and approved by him and that although he anticipated that cabinet officers would propose some modifications, the overall plan was set. I indicated that, speaking for OMB, we would be happy to entertain appeals but that I would not go along with any increases in any individual agency totals (a principle I ended up violating slightly in one instance). Don Regan also indicated that, speaking for the Budget Review Board,[22] it might be willing to

---

[22] Regan had established a three-person budget review board to hear appeals from agencies that were dissatisfied with OMB's final determinations. On it sat the chief of staff, the deputy chief of staff, and the president's national security adviser. Determinations by the budget review board could be appealed to the president either by the agency or by OMB.

entertain appeals from agencies for increases in their overall amounts but that any increase in one agency's amount would have to be offset by decreases in another agency's amount; those who asked for increases had better be prepared to make specific recommendations for cuts elsewhere. At that point, Sam Pierce, secretary of housing and urban development, asked jocularly, "Will those agencies who might be reduced further have an opportunity to express their views on priorities?"

Chatting with several cabinet officers after the meeting (and after retrieving copies of the books—again, to protect the innocent), I said, "Today marks a new chapter in my life: yesterday all agency heads were convinced I was their special friend; today, they all know I am their special enemy." (I was able to joke about this only because I perceived that the negative reaction was not as great as I had anticipated.)

The agencies react

Over the next week, we completed the appeals process. Most major agencies came back to OMB with suggestions for changes in their allotments (passbacks). My directions to the staff were to accommodate these changes when they were zero-sum—that is, when they did not increase the agency's overall budget—and when they did not conflict with the president's principles or the overall themes we had set forth for the 1987 budget. All these appeals were settled by OMB through extraordinary efforts by the associate directors and the deputy director— except six, four that went to the Budget Review Board and two that went to the president.

Initially, the Justice Department appealed, asking not only that the cuts we had made in their proposed budgets be restored but that it receive resources beyond those originally requested. The argument was that Justice was the "domestic defense" and therefore should be accorded something like the same treatment given to defense—that is, a hefty increase in real spending. Ed Meese made his pitch to the Budget Review Board, and, frankly, I tended to agree with some of the points he made. In the end, this matter was negotiated between Ed Meese's deputy, Lowell Jensen, and OMB associate director Carol Crawford. The result was to give the department $124 million more than we had given in passback but considerably less than the several hundred million dollars in additional resources the department had requested.

The new secretary of the Department of Health and Human Services (HHS), Dr. Otis Bowen, was sworn into office just before the week that budget appeals began. Over that weekend he called from Indiana and asked for a several-day postponement. I responded that because of the extraordinary delays created by the Gramm-Rudman-Hollings process and other events, we could not accommodate him. In the end, he came in and asked to appeal some of his budget to the Budget Review Board. Specifically, he did not request more funds but a rearrangement of the savings. He proposed that we relieve targeted caps on Medicare payments to doctors and capital reimbursement to hospitals in exchange for Medicare patients who could afford it paying front-end costs for hospital stays. Because the savings envisioned in these programs formed a substantial segment of our deficit reduction program, and because the new fees were analogous to taxes, we were reluctant to go along with Dr. Bowen's plan. Also, we thought it stood a much lower probability of being enacted than the one we had proposed.

Although I disagreed with Dr. Bowen's proposal, I must say I felt a kinship with him, having just taken over an agency and not yet having his feet on the ground. What was much more troubling, however, was that subsequently we began to see leaks about the president's budget for HHS on the front pages of the nation's newspapers. In particular, a front-page story in the Sunday *New York Times* characterized some of the cuts tentatively planned for the department in unflattering terms.[23] I called Dr. Bowen to let him know that, by the nature of the article, people in the White House were presuming the source of the leak was at HHS. He responded with some consternation and agreed to calm down his troops and reiterate the rules of the game.

The situation at the department was a difficult one because for the two years before Dr. Bowen's arrival much of the budgetary affairs of the department had been run by OMB. At the changing of the guard, departmental personnel saw an opportunity to get back at OMB and stand tall to impress the new arrival. In a letter to me about the appeal—a letter in all probability written for his signature—Dr. Bowen expressed concern over some of the policies, charging that they had been drafted by careerists at OMB and promoted only by them. The implication was that these proposals had not been reviewed by any of the president's people, only by career bureaucrats. In fact, the OMB budget proposals for the department had been reviewed not only by the political leadership of OMB but by the White House senior staff and the president himself! After a week of give and take with the department's budget people, we were finally able to conclude an acceptable compromise.

Two matters were appealed not only to the Budget Review Board but to the president. The first, of lesser import, was an appeal from the National Aeronautics and Space Administration (NASA). We had proposed slipping the space station development by three years and making other reductions in the agency's proposed budget. NASA accepted some of the cuts, asked for the restoration of monies in other areas, but was adamant that the space station development program reflected

---

[23] See Robert Pear, "Reagan's Budget for 1987 Seeking Medicare Savings," *New York Times*, December 15, 1985, p. A1.

a decision by the president, announced in the 1984 State of the Union Message, of putting a station into orbit and operation within a decade. It also reflected, according to NASA, earlier accords on space station funding: that after the various manned programs were complete the agency's budget would be reduced but thereafter would maintain a constant real rate of spending. At stake was some $400 million for 1987. NASA responded with yet another compromise that would have meant some cuts but kept the space station on track.

Despite my willingness to compromise, NASA insisted on going to the president on the matter of the space station. This, of course, irritated members of the Budget Review Board, who saw a way to compromise without involving the president and taking his time. Nevertheless, on December 20, NASA appealed to the president. Although a White House office was supposed to clear the NASA people through the White House security system, when the time arrived and the president stuck his head into the cabinet room to see if we were ready, the NASA people weren't there. They arrived some twenty minutes later to a chorus of apologies and assurances that there had been no plan to delay them.

Because NASA insisted in the restoration not only of the space station but of other monies as well, I decided to take the hard-line view of our original passback position in my presentation to the president. In the end, on the basis of an options paper drafted at OMB, the president chose to remain on schedule with the space station but accepted other aspects of the compromise that had earlier been rejected by NASA.

The other appeal to the president was by the Department of Defense. Here the major issue was whether the amount asked for in the 1987 budget should reflect the top line incorporated in the 1985 congressional budget resolution or whether the number should reflect simply a 3 percent in real growth for defense spending. In 1985, the president had asked for a 1986 budget for defense some 5.8 percent over the inflation rate—that's a 5.8 percent real increase. Eventually, he compromised on a 0 percent real increase for 1986 and a 3 percent real increase for 1987 and again for 1988. As it turned out, the inflation figures assumed for the 1986 budget were greater than appeared reasonable as we began putting together the 1987 budget. The major question, then, was whether the defense budget should reflect the realistic inflation rate or whether the president should ask for a top line reflecting an obsolete inflation rate—recognizing, of course, that in the end he would be forced to compromise on a lower figure.

The OMB position was that we had to go with 3 percent real growth for defense based on realistic inflation estimates. Besides, our estimate for the budget deficit for 1987 reflecting the passbacks to the agencies was close to the Gramm-Rudman-Hollings target of $144 billion. Thus, to accept the change would have meant our obtaining some $3 billion in cuts somewhere else.

Standard practice for appeals to the president had the agency officials who were appealing sit across the table from the president along with the OMB officials who would respond. When time came for the defense appeal, however, Cap Weinberger slipped around and sat down next to the president. Thus, when he made his argument, he was simply chatting with the president in casual, informal fashion, man to man. He also opened his book and shared with the president graphs, charts, and other information we did not have. In contrast, my presentation was from across the table, and I kept pulling things out of my book and handing them over to the president to illustrate the points I was trying to make. I had been "had," but I couldn't help but admire Cap's initiative. In the end, however, the president took the OMB position—to my surprise and great relief.

5 | The Gramm-Rudman-Hollings Fix

After the Supreme Court declared the automatic trigger mechanism of Gramm-Rudman-Hollings unconstitutional on July 7, 1986,[1] it became increasingly evident that without restoration of some kind of automatic device there would be little chance of making significant further progress on the deficit. With the Republican loss of the Senate in 1986, and with further developments in what became known as "Irangate,"[2] Congress became increasingly adversarial (as well as partisan) on budget issues. Basically, the Democratic leadership's attitude was that "we want additional programs, and we are willing to pay for them through higher taxes." The president's position, in contrast, was that "spending is too high already, and, furthermore, I will not increase taxes." (He was fond of pointing out that various studies had concluded that Congress tends to spend

---

[1] In *Bowsher v. Synar*, more commonly cited simply as *Synar*, the Supreme Court held that the Gramm-Rudman-Hollings trigger mechanism, which involved a decision by the comptroller general determining whether the president must order a sequester, violated the separation of powers doctrine inasmuch as the comptroller general is a subordinate of the Congress, not the president. Because of a separability provision in the act, the Supreme Court voided only the trigger mechanism, leaving the rest of Gramm-Rudman-Hollings intact. However, without an enforcement mechanism, Gramm-Rudman-Hollings was viewed by many as a toothless tiger.

[2] OMB associate executive director Tim Muris became fond of saying that the "Reagan revolution" ended in November 1986 with the revelation by President Reagan and Attorney General Ed Meese of Lt. Col. Oliver North's tactics to bolster the U.S. allies in Central America. Although this is an overstatement, primarily as a consequence of these developments, the final two years of the Reagan presidency were little more than a holding action against forces bent on undoing the president's reforms.

more than a dollar for each extra dollar raised in revenue.)[3] The result of the stalemate was that Congress inevitably would get its wish for more spending but that the president would prevail in taxes. What would give was progress on the deficit.

Some members of Congress and some officials in the administration—most notably Secretary of Defense Cap Weinberger and Secretary of State George Shultz—would have preferred seeing Gramm-Rudman-Hollings die or at least ignored. What they didn't count on was a determined group of senators, and arguably some members of congress, for whom getting the deficit under control was the number one priority and who, because of a quirk in the way we go about our fiscal affairs, possessed great leverage: by threatening to block yet another increase in the debt ceiling, they would eventually force a Gramm-Rudman-Hollings "fix."

The debt ceiling cliff

In 1987 a new element was present in the perennial debate over the debt ceiling. In October 1986, after considerable discussion over the Treasury Department's discretion in effectively stretching out the constraint imposed by a fixed debt ceiling (use of the federal financing bank, drawdown of balances, and so forth), Congress had made the debt ceiling a cliff. That is, on May 16, 1987, the debt ceiling would fall from $2.30 trillion to $2.11 trillion. This meant that, once the fall occurred, there was little the president could do to avoid bankruptcy for the federal government unless Congress acted within a matter of days, perhaps even hours.[4]

This represented an approach that, to my mind, considerably weakened the president's leverage. First, who wants to be president when the government goes belly up? Neither the international actors nor the U.S. citizens would hold anyone but the president responsible. Second, under the old debt ceiling arrangement, when the debt rose and then hit a plateau rather than falling off a cliff, the president arguably could cut back on spending unilaterally. That is, even though programs were appropriated, the debt ceiling would mean that he didn't have the wherewithal to pay for them. The question was whether the president

---

[3] For example, see Richard Vedder, Lowell Gallaway, and Christopher Frenze, "Federal Tax Increases and the Budget Deficit, 1957–1986," reprinted in *Congressional Record*, April 30, 1987, pp. S5754–55.

[4] Depending on the precise day the fall in the debt ceiling occurred, it might be possible for the U.S. government to avoid bankruptcy for a few days, so long as tax receipts held up and payments (outlays) were held in check.

had any discretion (could cut some programs and not others) or had to reduce spending by the same percentage across the board. If he could pick and choose among spending programs, this could see his priorities carried out and have enormous leverage with Congress.[5] But although the cliff took away the leverage the president might have had, it gave power to those who would hold out against an increase in the debt ceiling in exchange for whatever they wanted. And what they wanted was a Gramm-Rudman-Hollings fix.

The leverage held by these members of Congress and senators was greater than was generally imagined. As discussed in chapter 4, the consequence of not raising the debt ceiling was not just that the government would shut down but that it would go bankrupt. On May 15, Congress avoided a crisis by raising the debt ceiling to $2.32 billion and extending it through July 17; it later extended this limit through August 6. Thus, before adjourning for its August recess, Congress had to face up to extending the debt ceiling, for the cliff would be reached before Congress reconvened in September. In the meantime, proposals abounded for some sort of Gramm-Rudman-Hollings fix. House majority leader Tom Foley (D., Wash.), in keeping, he said, with the spirit of the original trigger mechanism, proposed that OMB, the Congressional Budget Office (CBO), and the General Accounting Office (GAO) forecast the coming year's deficit and then Congress would pass a law sequestering the amount necessary to hit the Gramm-Rudman-Hollings deficit targets. The onus would then be on the president to either accept the sequester law or veto it as he saw fit—an unpalatable position for the president.[6]

Senator Phil Gramm, in contrast, initially sought a simple constitutional fix to the automatic trigger mechanism: he would have CBO and GAO involved in the process but would leave it up to the director of OMB to make the final call as to whether a sequester were warranted. However, the OMB director's discretion would be severely limited. Not only would he have to explain in great detail any divergences between his final decisions and those recommended by CBO and GAO, but many of the assumptions (with respect to economic growth, unemployment, inflation rate, and so forth) were, in effect, to be legislated. The object was to make the OMB director perform a bookkeeping function, with no true authority.

---

[5] Such discriminating action, no doubt, would have precipitated numerous lawsuits and, in the minds of some, a constitutional crisis. Moreover, the administration's lawyers simply couldn't agree whether the president had such authority. Whether President Reagan would have ever chosen to exercise such authority is not known, though I raised it with him in person and in various memoranda.

[6] That is, Congress could take credit for reducing the deficit, and the president would be blamed for ordering cuts in spending.

After considerable hemming and hawing between the two bodies, the House finally gave up on the Foley proposal and sent over to the Senate a clean debt ceiling bill, extending the cliff for thirty days. But would the Senate accept this? A handful of Republican senators, led by Gramm and Bill Armstrong (R., Colo.), dug in their heels. They refused to allow passage of a debt ceiling bill without a Gramm-Rudman-Hollings fix, and they believed they had the necessary votes to prevent *cloture* (an initiative to force a vote on the measure). In short, they were prepared to filibuster the debt ceiling, even though this threatened to bankrupt the U.S. government and to hold their colleagues past the vacation hour.

In early August, Howard Baker (the president's new chief of staff) and I visited with Gramm, Armstrong, and others in Bob Dole's (R., Kans.) office. What was said or promised in that meeting has been subject to some differences of interpretation. But my recollection was that the administration tentatively agreed to accept some kind of reasonable Gramm-Rudman-Hollings fix on the next debt ceiling bill provided those Republican senators call off their threatened filibuster. Baker indicated that he was not authorized to make a final commitment on the spot but that the two of us would raise it with the president for his reaction. We adjourned the meeting and returned to the White House; shortly thereafter Baker and I met with the president and presented him with this deal, which he accepted. We then notified Dole, Gramm, Armstrong, and the others.

Almost immediately, we began a series of meetings to discuss how best to address this matter when Congress returned from its August vacation. It was agreed that I would convene a group of second-tier officials to develop a specific strategy, which I did. In a couple of days we had banged out a good plan that involved important budget process reforms in addition to a Gramm-Rudman-Hollings fix. These included votes on the line-item veto, balanced budget constitutional amendments,[7] converting the congressional budget resolution into a binding budget law, and several other highly desirable reforms.

The president's senior advisers reconvened to discuss the next steps. We all generally agreed with the goals of the draft strategy report that had been distributed earlier. But as to tactics, there was considerable disagreement. I was in favor of a direct approach—that is, negotiating directly with Congress over budget process reforms as well as the Gramm-Rudman-Hollings fix.

The rest, however, argued strenuously for a more behind-the-scenes approach—letting our allies on Capitol Hill carry the ball. They argued, persuasively I thought, that budget process reform was a Hill issue and that we would have little influence, being seen as outsiders. Another advantage was that this would

---

[7] The major threshold on these items was getting a vote on the floor of the House of Representatives. The House leadership thus far had refused to allow such a vote over concern that the resolutions would pass with the necessary two-thirds majority.

allow the major protagonists to have their fight and end up compromising with their Hill opponents, thus keeping the president from looking as though he were opposed to deficit reduction.

The upshot of the meeting was that we would try the more indirect approach and see what developed. Shortly thereafter, there commenced a series of meetings with congressional Republicans—particularly with task forces set up by the minority leaders of the two Houses. After some discussion, we all agreed on a set of goals encompassing most of the budget process reforms we had advocated plus a Gramm-Rudman-Hollings fix that generally comported with our major objective, which was meeting the Gramm-Rudman-Hollings target for 1988 without a sequester.

After a long series of direct negotiations among members of Congress and lengthy telephone conversations involving several officials of the administration, the Senate passed a Gramm-Rudman-Hollings fix that paid little more than lip service to budget process reform but that was generally acceptable. I felt confident that the president would endorse this approach because I felt I could assure him (as well as Cap Weinberger and George Shultz) that a sequester would not result, at least for 1988. Because the House had earlier passed a clean debt ceiling, the matter now went to conference. With a feeling bordering on elation, I looked forward to this conference's adopting the Senate version, both Houses passing it, and sending it to the president.

To my surprise and consternation, the House conferees insisted on changing the Senate version. First, they would not accept even the puny budget process reforms—credit reform and accounting of outlays for the House[8]—that were contained in the Senate bill. In short, they would accept nothing that would make the budget more efficient, effective, or predictable. Moreover, the House wanted to lower the deficit targets, disallow asset sales from deficit reduction computations, and force a sequester.

This was a repeat of the 1985 episode. The way the Democrats saw it, there were two possible, politically attractive outcomes. One was the chance that, with a compulsory sequester, the president might veto the bill, in which case they would have gained an enormous political advantage by having the president appear to be against reducing the deficit. But what they really wanted was to force the president to accept higher taxes. They had seen the president oppose tax measures many times before but in the end accept them. They thought he would do the same thing again.

---

[8] Under the Budget and Accounting Act of 1974, the Senate had to establish targets for outlays in addition to budget authority for discretionary spending, but the House did not. This exception allowed the House to play games with budgeting (see discussion in chapter 10).

What they didn't realize was that the president was more resolved than ever before to oppose a tax increase on the grounds that tax increases simply increased the size, scope, and interference of the government and led to no reduction in the deficit. The president often mentioned that the 1982 tax legislation had been sold to him on the basis that for every dollar increase in revenue, there would be a three-dollar reduction in spending. He believed he had gotten the increase in revenue and an *increase*, not a decrease, in spending. Hence, he wasn't going to be suckered into that kind of position again.

While this House-Senate conference was going on, I stayed in touch with three individuals: first, my old friend Phil Gramm; second, Senate Budget Committee ranking member Pete Domenici (R., N. Mex.); and third, House minority whip Trent Lott (R., Miss.). Lott's position was that the threat of a sequester for defense was so significant that he would prefer not to have a Gramm-Rudman-Hollings fix—that is, he would prefer to fight out the domestic spending programs and the tax increase on their own merits. Domenici's position was that the Senate-passed version made sense and that we should work toward that end.

Throughout the discussions with Phil, Pete, and Trent, I repeated my own assessment that a Gramm-Rudman-Hollings fix that forced another sequester—with its direct hit on defense—would be difficult for the president to swallow. I told them confidentially that I knew that Cap Weinberger and George Shultz would argue feverishly against it and that the president himself would be angered should he be forced to choose between a tax increase and cutting defense. My reading of the matter was vindicated when the president's decision to sign what became known as "Gramm-Rudman-Hollings II" was a damn close thing.

Problems with the fix

In late September, both Houses passed the compromise conference report, which required a $23 billion sequester for 1988, and sent it to President Reagan. Incredibly, members of Congress had passed a major initiative they really couldn't fathom. I know this to be true because, despite having the best and the brightest in the Budget Review Division of OMB, we were unable to understand the bill fully in all its details. In some areas the legislative language contained outright contradictions. In other areas, there was a great deal of ambiguity, and it was difficult to understand the intent of Congress as to how the law would apply.

Despite working over the weekend, around the clock, and evaluating several different versions of the legislative language, by Monday we were still unable to give the president a thorough, concrete assessment of the fix and how it would work. On the morning of Wednesday, September 23, Howard Baker called and said that the president wished to discuss with Jim Baker, Cap Weinberger, and me the Gramm-Rudman-Hollings fix. I would be expected to present an overview.

Later that day we all met in the Oval Office. I started off by saying that Congress had just passed a fixed-up Gramm-Rudman-Hollings (now known as Gramm-Rudman-Hollings II) and that, briefly, its pluses were as follows: it extended the debt ceiling into 1989 (thus avoiding a fight over this issue during the election year of 1988); it recommitted the U.S. government to deficit reduction, thus having positive effects on the economy; it would keep the president out front on the deficit reduction issue; and it would greatly ease the preparation of our 1989 budget (having as a deficit target $136 billion instead of $72 billion).[9] I also told him that a majority of Republicans supported the bill and that there was no assurance that he would be able to sustain a veto of the measure. Moreover, I pointed out that enactment would avoid the prospect of the federal government's going bankrupt.

I also pointed out the measure's minuses: it contained a compulsory sequester, which meant a big hit on defense; it would put pressure on the president to increase taxes (to avoid the hit on defense); and many opportunities had been missed to cut domestic spending and to reform the budget process. I also mentioned some strange, objectionable provisions such as expedited procedures for congressional consideration of deficit reduction alternatives proposed by the majority leaders in both Houses but none for alternatives proposed by the minority leaders or by the president! I also told him that we didn't get all we had demanded, which went to the matter of our credibility. And finally, I indicated, on the basis of previous telephone calls to the GOP leadership, that I could not assure him of veto strength on either the upcoming reconciliation bill or the continuing resolution.

The president listened politely to the pluses of the measure, but when I began to hit the minuses, particularly my comments about the pressures on defense and taxes, he began shaking his head and getting red in the face.

Then Cap Weinberger made his presentation, and it was a doozer. Cap said that signing the bill would mean the compulsory discharge of 400,000 uniformed personnel and 150,000 reservists. Cap argued that even though Gramm-Rudman-Hollings had been in existence for more than a year, progress on the deficit had been minimal.[10] Finally, Cap cautioned the president that signing the bill would put him in a deficit versus taxes box.

Jim Baker then took the floor and urged the president to sign the bill to

---

[9] Under the old Gramm-Rudman-Hollings law, the president was required to *submit* a budget for 1989 meeting a $72 billion deficit target and Congress was required to *pass* a budget meeting that target. However, as mentioned earlier, following the *Synar* decision by the Supreme Court, there could be no sequester.

[10] Cap was especially wrong on this count: the deficit was in the process of falling a record $71 billion—from $221 billion in 1986 to $150 billion in 1987.

prevent the U.S. government's going into receivership.[11] He argued that although opportunities did exist for Congress to pass a clean debt ceiling (that is, separate from a Gramm-Rudman-Hollings fix), it was unlikely to do so.

However, it was clear to all of us sitting in the room that the president was not persuaded that he should sign the bill and in fact was leaning strongly against it. Moreover, he expressed such strong sentiment against the bill and against those in Congress who were trying to put him in a box, that I was a bit afraid that he was going to take off a few heads, with mine the first in line.

The president adjourned the meeting, and several of us (not including Weinberger) retired to discuss the situation. All of us agreed that the president should sign the bill, gritting his teeth. But how to get him to do that, given his state of mind? We all agreed that at the present moment, the president would say no, so we didn't want to press the issue. Also, an interesting discussion arose as to the proper role of a presidential aide. Some said the role of a presidential aide is to prevent the president from doing the wrong thing. I, in contrast, stated that the appropriate role of a presidential aide is to present the president with facts on which he might make a decision and to express one's views but to leave it at that. Once the president has made a decision, the aide's responsibility is to carry it out—provided it's lawful.

Later, Howard Baker went to see the president about the matter, and after a brief discussion the president said he would think about it. He agreed to review three pieces of paper, all of which I was to prepare: first, a memorandum summarizing the pros and cons; second, a draft veto message; and third, a draft signing message.

The next day (September 24), the GOP leaders came down to visit with the president in the Oval Office. The subject was Gramm-Rudman-Hollings II. The president opened the session by saying, "Why don't you simply send me a clean debt ceiling bill?" The first leader[12] responded that they were too far down the road to back up now and that the president could veto the continuing resolution if he didn't get what he wanted for defense. The president said that if he signed the bill we'd go back to the defense levels of the early 1980s.[13] That same leader responded that the Republicans could, in fact, sustain a veto of the continuing resolution, if that's what the president wanted.

---

[11] Jim Baker was particularly strong in his advocacy on this point, perhaps reflecting that, under current law, the secretary of the Treasury is *personally* liable for the debts of the U.S. government!

[12] Because this was a freewheeling, off-the-record-discussion, I will not identify the GOP leaders by name. To do so would betray confidences.

[13] This wasn't exactly true, but this was what, no doubt, he recalled Cap's having told him.

The second leader said that he personally could not support an effort to sustain a veto of Gramm-Rudman-Hollings II, even though it was hard for him to say that. He said that the Democrats would lay snares for the Republicans in 1988. The place to do the work on defense was in the appropriations bills and on taxes was in the reconciliation bill.

The third leader pointed out the importance of extending the debt limit to 1989. Also, he suggested that we were getting more in this bill than we had a right to expect. He urged us to think about this as merely the opening wedge, that the fight was only now beginning. He argued that the Democrats didn't want a sequester either but that the White House had to get involved in the reconciliation fight if a tax increase were to be avoided. He suggested that the Republicans would be able to sustain vetoes of any individual appropriations bills that exceeded the president's budget by a "buck fifty-nine" ($1.59).

The fourth leader, who had personally assured me before the Senate floor debate on Gramm-Rudman-Hollings II that he could in good conscience vote no as well as yes, suggested that the president had no choice. He said that signing or vetoing the measure wouldn't change the ultimate defense appropriation, but he suggested that the president let the tension build. The fifth leader also argued that this was simply the opening round and that even if we had a sequester it would at least reduce spending on a number of undesirable domestic programs. The sixth leader argued that the president should sign the bill—that Gramm-Rudman-Hollings had led to substantial deficit reduction and that with a veto the Republicans would lose the issue and chaos would ensue.

The third leader then pointed out that if the president were to sustain a veto of Gramm-Rudman-Hollings II, it would be with the strangest assortment of folks you ever saw—conservative Republicans following the president and "a bunch of left-wing kooks" who simply didn't like anything that cut spending.

The president is not happy

This show of unity on the part of the GOP leadership and the remote possibility of sustaining a veto of Gramm-Rudman-Hollings II clearly affected the president. Until then, I think he had been thinking that the possibilities of having a veto of the measure sustained and forcing Congress to pass a simple debt limit extension were fairly good. But the GOP leaders' message dashed those hopes.

It was arguably now a matter of the president's coming around to this conclusion on his own. Accordingly, I hastened to prepare the formal decision memorandum (as well as the two draft messages), hoping the president would indicate his decision without much fanfare. The president, however, surprised us all by deciding to give more thought to the matter. With the clock ticking, the situation with respect to the debt ceiling was getting desperate. It was generally concluded that the president would have to make his decision known that weekend and that the Saturday radio address (September 26) seemed a logical place for him to communicate his decision.

For the rest of the week everyone was on pins and needles, not knowing which way the president would go. I personally indicated to several of my associates that if I were in the president's shoes, I would do exactly what he was doing—keeping everyone in suspense. Numerous calls from the Hill were responded to with "I don't know" or "I don't know any more than you do." Some people were getting desperate, most especially Jim Baker.

That weekend was one that I had set aside for a rare trip to our mountain cabin, and I had endeavored to leave with my family early on Friday afternoon to beat the traffic out of Washington. But I wanted to look over the draft of the president's Saturday address, not only to see whether he was planning to sign the bill or veto it but to check it for facts and tone. Just before leaving, I asked someone to bring the closely guarded copy over, and we sat down and reviewed the draft one final time. One sentence was worded so that the president seemed to be agreeing to accept a tax increase! I indicated that this had to be changed. Another sentence raised a factual question, which I asked some members of my staff to check out, and this too was changed. So, at 1:07 on Saturday afternoon, standing beside my radio at the cabin, I heard the president say he would sign the measure, albeit with considerable misgivings.

On the following Tuesday, September 29, the president held a signing ceremony in the Rose Garden. Early in the day I had received a copy of his draft remarks and had read it carefully. As I had predicted, it was a statement that indicated he was signing the bill only with great reluctance and that scolded Congress for giving him such bad choices. In one place the president noted that some in Congress thought they had put him in a box between taxes and defense. He went on to recall the incident in World War II during the Battle of the Bulge when an American general and his troops were surrounded; to a demand that the general surrender he replied with one word: "Nuts." The next few lines in the draft read something to the effect that those who thought the president would go along with cutting defense or raising taxes were wrong. I made a slight change in the text so that the passage read, "To those who say we must weaken America's defenses: They're nuts. To those who say we must raise the tax burden on the American people: They, too, are nuts." I liked this new version; it was more forceful, and I had no doubt that if the president read that line it would become the "sound byte" that appeared on the evening's network news shows. But I didn't think it would get past the speech writers, much less past the president.

During the afternoon ceremony, my position was on the front row at the right end. You can imagine my surprise and delight when, standing there looking over the president's shoulder, I saw that, in the next lines after the story about the general, that he had kept the speech as I had amended it. And, as I had anticipated, that was the sound byte that led the network news shows that evening.

But the president also gave a stern lecture that day. He began his remarks by saying, "Bill signing moments are usually happy events. This one is not." Noting that a host of congressional leaders were standing beside and behind me, I felt they must have been uneasy with the president speaking to them in those tones. Later, Howard Baker asked me what I thought of the ceremony, and I told him I thought it was good and appropriate that the president indicate his sentiments about the matter. Baker told me that he had been "positively scared" that one or more of those congressional leaders were going to bolt the session because of being dressed down so severely.

Thus, Gramm-Rudman-Hollings II became a reality. The next step was how to avoid a sequester without a tax increase, a task arguably made easier by the promise of the GOP leaders that they would support a veto of excessive appropriations—a pledge that I reinforced by mentioning it to several of them as they were leaving the White House after the signing ceremony. As we will see in the next chapter, this strategy was to prove irrelevant.

6 | Black Monday

On Monday, October 19, 1987, I had a reasonably light schedule, punctuated with a lunch and a speech on transportation deregulation at the National Press Club. Somehow, this had been scheduled for a Monday, so I was to miss the president's issues luncheon, which I regularly attended.

An ominous note marked urgent

Around 11:00 in the morning, someone from my press office came in my outer office and left a note with a copy of an Associated Press story. The note, marked urgent, said the Dow-Jones Industrial index was off 69 points in heavy trading. The story also reported that gold had risen in New York and that thirty-year Treasury bonds had fallen some $20, as yield had risen to nearly 10.4 percent. This was disconcerting news, though not totally unexpected. The previous week the market had closed down substantially in the last three days of trading: off 95, 57, and 108 points, respectively (see figure 6).

For those of us who had been following economic activity, the slide in the stock market was no surprise. For months, Beryl Sprinkel (chairman of the Council of Economic Advisers) and I had been sounding the alarm internally over the Federal Reserve Board's (Fed's) highly restrictive monetary policy. After a two-year period in which the money aggregates had grown at rates substantially above those needed to maintain full employment, beginning in 1987 the Fed had held M1 and, especially, M1A, virtually frozen.[1]

---

[1] M1 is the sum of the nation's currency, demand deposits, travelers checks, and other checkable deposits. M1A is M1 *minus* other checkable deposits.

Figure 6:   Dow-Jones, Week before Black Monday

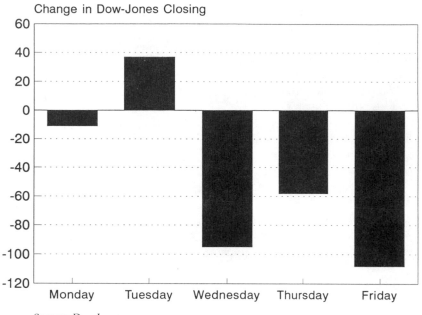

Change in Dow-Jones Closing

SOURCE: Dow-Jones

Although the matter is complicated, in the two previous years the Fed had maintained a policy that, in normal times, would have generated an inflation rate of approximately 4 percent. In 1986, however, the oil cartel broke down, prices fell, and supplies increased substantially. Because energy is such a large part of our economy and consequently constitutes a large component of the price indexes, this development slowed the rate of inflation. For example, the consumer price index (CPI) rose only 1.1 percent over the period December 1986 to December 1987.

In the spring of 1987, however, the cartel pieced itself back together, re-strained supplies, and oil prices rose. Then, instead of experiencing an inflation rate of approximately 4 percent, which Fed policy would have generated in normal times, the monthly inflation figures (expressed as annual rates) rose to approxi-mately 6 percent. The Fed panicked and stepped hard on the brakes.

Monetary policy affects real economic activity with a *distributed lag*, mean-ing that the effects on the economy begin some six or eight months after the monetary action and last as long as eighteen months, with the major impact coming a year or so after the initial policy change. Beginning in the early spring, then, Sprinkel and I discussed our concerns with Secretary of Treasury Jim Baker and Secretary of State George Shultz at our weekly Tuesday breakfasts hosted by Baker. (Also usually in on the conversation was Commerce Secretary Malcolm Baldrige.) Unfortunately, Sprinkel and I were unable to make many inroads with Baker and Shultz on this matter, and Baker was the one who dealt directly with Fed chairman Paul Volcker on behalf of the administration. As the spring gave way to summer, Baker began to share our concerns but argued that it wasn't possible to address the situation until Volcker (whose term was about to expire) had left his post.

There is a simple, but useful, adage: stock market levels reflect information about real economic activity, whereas market variability reflects the psychology of the moment. It is also true, though, that the market tends to anticipate economic trends and so is looked on by many as a "leading indicator."

Given the circumstances, that the stock market continued to rise through August surprised me, for it was becoming apparent that the Fed's monetary policies were raising the specter of a recession during late 1987 or early 1988. Back in April 1987, I had mentioned my concern about this problem during a breakfast attended by a host of Washington reporters. The result was a front-page story in the *New York Times*,[2] reporting my comments and speculating that mine was just the first salvo in an administration effort to blame the Fed for any economic downturn. Controversy over this report led the nervous Nellies at the Western White House (the president was in California) to issue a statement to the effect that, in the president's judgment, the Fed was pursuing a perfectly sensible course on the economy.

Unfortunately, the Fed's policies were not all the bad news coming out of Washington. During the week leading up to "Black Monday," both the Senate Finance and the House Ways and Means committees marked up reconciliation bills that would have raised tax revenue over $12 billion during 1988 and more each year thereafter. Many of these tax initiatives were aimed directly at corporations—specifically, their ability to respond to market opportunities. That week also saw Judge Robert Bork's nomination to the Supreme Court defeated on the floor of the Senate. Suspicion grew that the president not only had lost any chance he had to gain approval of his legislative program but would be unable to block major legislation with which he disagreed.[3] Also, during the latter part of the

---

[2] "U.S. Budget Chief Opposes Increase in Interest Rates," *New York Times*, April 17, 1987. This breakfast was a weekly series organized by former *Christian Science Monitor* Washington bureau chief Godfrey Sperling. The Sperling Breakfast series goes back to October 1966, and by tradition, the president attends one each year.

[3] Of particular concern was the potpourri of protectionist trade measures that had passed both Houses and were then in conference.

week and especially on the weekend news shows, Jim Baker, en route to Europe, criticized some of our major trading partners—especially the Germans—for maintaining restrictive fiscal policies and for trying to inflate the dollar (thus worsening our balance of trade). Last, but not least, during the early morning hours of Black Monday, U.S. forces took out two Iranian sea platforms on which were mounted various surveillance gear enabling the Iranians to monitor the activities of ships in the Persian Gulf.[4]

Because of the stock market's behavior the previous week, the substantial early-morning drop in the Dow-Jones index gave rise to serious concerns on the part of government officials. Telephone calls among major players were frequent, even before lunch. Beryl Sprinkel indicated he would bring the president up to date on his views at the issues luncheon. Just before noon, I walked over to the cabinet room, thinking that this topic would be number one on the agenda and that I would participate in the discussion before going over to the National Press Club and giving my address. Unfortunately, the Office of Cabinet Affairs (which set the agenda) had chosen to put the economy at the end of the session (discussion of the morning's military action was to precede), so I left OMB deputy director Joe Wright at the luncheon and went over to the Press Club.

The discussion during lunch was dominated by news about the market, but there was talk of transportation issues as well. Concerned that one of the transportation reporters might ask me about the market, I left the table briefly to call the office. My staff reported the market had been down as far as 150 points but had rebounded to only (!) 128 points down.

Fortunately, no one asked me about the market in the question-and-answer session following my luncheon address, but on my way out of the building I was dragooned by reporters from the Cable News Network for a statement. I responded that in my view the market's decline had been irrational, and I noted approvingly that the Dow-Jones index had already begun to rebound.

On returning to the office, I found that the market was then down some 200 points and "heading south"! I immediately called Beryl, only to be told he was "over in the West Wing." I ran over to Howard Baker's office and found Baker, Sprinkel, and a few others discussing the situation. (Jim Baker was still in Europe.) They had urged the Fed's new chairman, Alan Greenspan, to make a statement indicating the Fed's willingness to "assure liquidity" and "stand behind the nation's economic system." Greenspan, however, had contacted members of the Fed's

---

[4] The Iranians had just sunk a U.S. flagged tanker in Kuwaiti waters. How to respond to the Iranians had been discussed extensively at a National Security Council meeting the previous week. Indeed, I had visited with National Security adviser Frank Carlucci to discuss options on Saturday, October 17, just before leaving for our cabin for the remainder of the weekend.

Open Market Committee, and they had agreed, unanimously, that no such statement should be issued. Greenspan, in fact, was en route to Dallas, where he was to give a speech to the American Bankers Association.

The situation was not good. The two major financial leaders of our government were out of touch. Demands abounded from every corner of the land for us to do something to end this mess. And the market kept falling. What impressed me most at this meeting, however, was the full understanding that most things the government might do would make the situation worse, not better.

In the early afternoon, Securities and Exchange Commission chairman David Ruder, responding to the press, ticked off a number of actions the commission might take, *including* closing the stock market. This, arguably, set off a new wave of panic selling, for the market quickly developed a "free-fall" condition. Later in the day, the president issued a statement (through Marlin Fitzwater) that he had directed consultations among officials of the administration, the heads of the New York, Chicago, and Los Angeles exchanges, and other leaders of the investment community. Marlin reported that "those consultations confirm our view that the underlying economy remains sound." President Reagan reiterated this position in his departure from Bethesda Naval Hospital (where the first lady had undergone surgery for breast cancer), remarking, "I don't think anyone should panic, because all the economic indicators are solid."

Of course, in retrospect, the single most important failure of Black Monday was the Federal Reserve's not rising to the occasion. In retrospect, had the Fed responded affirmatively in any positive way at all, I believe the market would not have experienced the collapse of 508 points in one day[5] (see figure 7).

The morning after

The next morning began an important day for me because under the recently passed Gramm-Rudman-Hollings fix (Gramm-Rudman-Hollings II), I had to report to the president and Congress the cuts that would be made in domestic and defense spending should there be a sequester. I began the day by attending a Sperling Breakfast that had been scheduled weeks earlier. Although in meeting with reporters I tried to focus on the Gramm-Rudman-Hollings report, I knew that a major portion of the discussion would be on the stock market. In my responses to questions, I kept emphasizing the theme of the president's remarks the previous evening—that the underlying economy was sound. I also repeated

---

[5] This is not to say the Fed caused Black Monday; I do believe, however, that the Fed failed to act with due dispatch to mitigate its severity.

Figure 7: Dow-Jones, Week of Black Monday

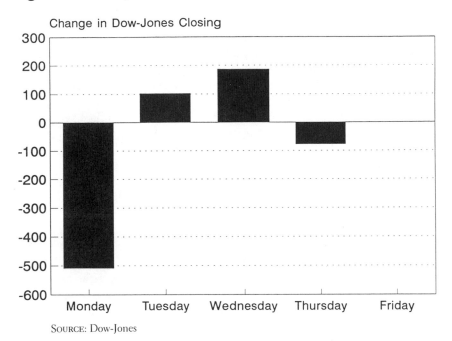

Change in Dow-Jones Closing

Source: Dow-Jones

a recurring theme of the administration: President Reagan was determined to veto any tax increase or protectionist trade legislation should it reach his desk.

The next stop was the Oval Office, where I presented the president with the Gramm-Rudman-Hollings report and the initial sequester order that, by law, he was required to sign. When I told him why I was there, his response was, "Oh shucks." I knew that the president disdained the whole notion of a sequester. And, according to this report, unless Congress came up with some $13 billion in savings, the president would have to order some $23 billion in across-the-board spending cuts—half from defense and half from domestic programs. Although the president signed the report, he again indicated his desire to avoid a sequester if at all possible. I interjected, "But without taxes, Mr. President?" "Without taxes," he affirmed.

Next, I headed for the White House briefing room, where I was to make a presentation on the Gramm-Rudman-Hollings report and its consequences. Just as I was beginning my presentation I was handed a note saying, "Marlin says do not say anything about the stock market." Of course, that was impossible, for surely there would be questions about the market's performance over the previous several days. I did what I could, however, to deflect such questions, and mercifully there were reasonably few that required a direct answer. But in all my responses, I fell back on the president's statements and the principles we had agreed on, especially our opposition to a tax increase. Also, I pointed out the progress we were making on the deficit under Gramm-Rudman-Hollings. I even suggested that the most underreported story of 1987 was that the deficit had fallen by one-third—from $221 billion in fiscal year 1986 to what we were estimating to be $148 billion in the year just ended.

Bill Gray (D., Pa.), chairman of the House Budget Committee, had asked me to testify on the Gramm-Rudman-Hollings report beginning at 11:00 A.M., so I promptly headed to Capitol Hill. When I arrived, the committee had not yet assembled, so Bill invited me back to his office for a private discussion. There, he stressed to me the importance of avoiding a sequester. "This is not an ideological thing, nor is it a partisan matter," said Bill. "We've got to do something." I agreed and indicated a willingness to discuss alternatives. Bill suggested we try to keep the hearing fairly nonpartisan; I agreed.

But the hearing opened with repeated partisan attacks on the president, and, because it was being broadly televised, I concluded I had to defend him in no uncertain terms. It developed into the most adversarial hearing I attended while director of OMB.

Throughout, I was pummeled by Democrats who derided Jim Baker for his comment on the previous Sunday's "Meet the Press" suggesting that the Democrats' tax proposal might have been partially responsible for the stock market's ending the week in a downturn. The Democrats retorted that the blame for the previous week and for Black Monday must be placed squarely at the feet of the president for his refusal to meet with the Democratic leadership to solve the deficit problem. And, incidentally, they said, such a set of negotiations would have to be with "no preconditions," with "everything on the table" (code words for the president must be willing not only to accept a tax increase but to sponsor it). Following the script we had all agreed on for months, I opposed the notion of an "economic summit" as well as a tax increase. Hour after hour it went on. The Democrats: "The president is the cause of the problem, because he won't meet with the leaders of Congress" (and increase taxes); me: "No, the problem is not the president, and he won't meet with you if it means raising taxes."

A change of direction?

While I was still on Capitol Hill, Howard Baker called a meeting in his office that included Jim Baker (who had returned from Europe the previous evening), Alan Greenspan, and Beryl Sprinkel. That meeting was later transferred to the Treasury Department and finally to the president's residence. But when I returned from the Hill, rather than learning about that extraordinary meeting with the president involving the future course of our policy toward spending and taxes, I went to a previously planned briefing by OMB staff and then adjourned to an especially scheduled briefing on the Department of Defense's *black programs*—that part of the budget covering top-secret research and weapons systems such as the B-2 stealth bomber.

Whether I was systematically excluded from that meeting with the president, I shall never know. In response to numerous press inquiries—offered to be on background or even off the record—I continued to express a doubt that this was intentional. "After all, I was testifying on the Hill at the time the meeting was called." As time progressed and patterns of behavior became more evident, however, I concluded that there had been little enthusiasm for my being involved in this meeting because I thought the deficit had little to do with the market's recent plunge; I thought little would be gained (and much lost) by the president's meeting with the congressional leadership, much less consummating a deal; I still strongly opposed any tax increase; and I might well have been able to persuade the president to "stay the course."

While I was in the secret briefing, a member of my public affairs staff inquired whether I would accept an invitation to go on the "MacNeil/Lehrer NewsHour" that evening. I thought it wise to avoid public debate on the stock market because during the day, following a brief but important statement of support by the Fed (which was initiated, in part, by the Department of the Treasury), the market had recovered a couple of hundred points (see figure 7). Unfortunately, it seemed impossible to avoid discussing the market the way the program was being set up. I called the White House Communications Office for advice. The head of the office suggested I not go on the show unless the format could be contained; he also mentioned, somewhat offhandedly, that the president would be issuing a statement at any moment.

Shortly thereafter I returned to my office to catch the president on television as he was departing for Bethesda Naval Hospital. He read a short statement indicating that he had "just finished a meeting with his economic advisers." He also noted that he had just signed the Gramm-Rudman-Hollings sequester report but that he thought it was "preferable, if possible, that the executive and legislative branches reach agreement on a deficit reduction package." "Accordingly," he said, he was "directing that discussions be undertaken with the bipartisan leadership of the Congress for that purpose." He was then asked whether this meant he would entertain a tax increase. His response was ambiguous—something to the effect that he would wait and see what they sent him. I immediately called Howard Baker and asked for an explanation. He said that the president's last words were not in his statement and that I should not presume there were any hidden meanings. In the meantime, MacNeil/Lehrer had agreed to a format that would allow me to go on the show and focus on budget matters, not the stock market.

Thus, I immediately obtained a copy of the president's remarks and took off for the local Public Broadcast Station television studio in Arlington, Virginia. Armed with the president's statement, his well-known opposition to a tax increase, and Howard Baker's assurances, I went on the program and contested with Bill Gray (the other panelist) the notion that the president would agree to a tax increase (or that he should). I also suggested that the president's statement was a call not for a full-fledged congressional summit but for negotiations over an alternative to a sequester—something the president had been saying he wanted for several weeks.

The next morning at the 8:00 White House operations meeting, Howard Baker conveyed to all of us, in strong terms, that the president's comment of the previous evening had not telegraphed his position on taxes—or, for that matter, his position on a full-blown congressional summit. Moreover, shortly after the meeting, Howard assured me that there had been no change in plans and that a tax increase was not in the works. He did, however, suggest that because the president had said something on the record, we must be sensitive about seeming to be correcting him. I agreed.

In response to the president's direction that we meet with the congressional leadership to find a way of avoiding a sequester, we were scheduled on Capitol Hill later that morning to visit with House minority leader Bob Michel, Senate majority leader Bob Byrd, Senate minority leader Bob Dole, and House Speaker Jim Wright, in that order.

But before the visits on the Hill, I stopped off at a local hotel to give a previously scheduled speech to the board of directors of the Council of Better Business Bureaus. Not surprisingly, several television stations covered the event. Although my speech was generally about the budget, in response to an inquiry about whether the president would agree to a tax increase, I offered my opinion that the president would not—that should the Congress send him a tax increase he would veto it. This remark was widely quoted, and a tape was shown on at least one network evening news program. The comment received special attention because that afternoon some anonymous White House spokespersons were conveying to the press the message that the president was indeed willing to consider a tax increase.

Shortly thereafter, when the president's representatives visited with Bob Michel, Howard Baker indicated that he and Jim Baker—but specifically not Jim Miller—had been invited to meet with the Speaker. Shocked by this, I asked what was going on. His response was that, for some reason, the Speaker was not particularly fond of me. I indicated it was bad form for anyone to be dictating whom the president might choose as his negotiators; Howard agreed, and after some calls the Speaker relented.

Next were meetings with Bob Byrd and Bob Dole, including the customary photo sessions. Jim Baker and I had lunch in the Senate dining room and discussed the Gramm plan of freezing domestic spending or holding it to no more than the percentage increase allowed for defense. We also discussed other approaches to avoiding a sequester.

We met with the Speaker in the afternoon. Initially it was a generally cordial affair, but at one point the Speaker began to complain bitterly about spending cuts that had already been made. The question came to me to describe by how much. I responded that the domestic appropriations bills marked up by the House were almost 5 percent above the current year's levels and some 15 percent above the president's request. This prompted the Speaker to go on an emotional tirade about how "year after year after year" domestic spending had been cut, while defense spending had grown out of control. He went on about the matter for a long period. As I was to learn, the Speaker was prone to use me as a means of venting his strong criticisms of the president's position without attacking the president.

The remainder of the meeting was devoted to the major preliminaries of the negotiations (when, where, and with whom). At the end, however, the Speaker made it plain that he expected the president to go along with a tax increase.

Although it is difficult to explain variations—even broad variations—in the stock market with simple events, I think it is no coincidence that my strong statements of Tuesday morning opposing a tax increase, my statement on the "MacNeil/Lehrer NewsHour" Tuesday evening, and my widely reported remarks of Wednesday morning accompanied a substantial recovery of the market. In fact, after the 508-point drop on Monday, the market recovered 102 points on Tuesday and 187 more points on Wednesday[6] (see figure 7).

On Thursday, however, the market faltered and ended the day with a 77-point loss. Part of the reason, I believe, is that word began circulating that the president had agreed to a full-blown congressional summit with taxes on the table. With increasing media attention to the budget deficit as the source of the market's instability and, in turn, the president's seeming intransigence, some of his senior advisers panicked. Another meeting was called—from which I was again excluded—to assess the situation and to press on the president the need to go along with a congressional summit even if it meant an increase in taxes. Had I attended the meeting I would have argued vociferously that the perception the president and Congress were "finally working together" would have no more effect on markets than Tweedledum or Tweedledee and that the president would be foolish to give up his position on taxes on the basis of such a faulty, psychological explanation of the situation.

Throughout the day on Thursday, White House staff sent frantic messages

---

[6] Of course, another major element was the Fed's statement of Tuesday morning saying it would support the financial markets.

to the media, claiming that the president was "flexible," that he would, indeed, be willing to meet with the congressional leadership with no preconditions. In fact, the staff drafted a statement, to be issued in the name of the president, which said exactly that: he would welcome meeting with the congressional leadership and that everything (save Social Security) would be put on the table—a clear indication he would go along with a tax increase. Asked about this development while departing for the hospital to visit the first lady, the president hemmed and hawed but indicated that he would still strongly argue against a tax increase.

Should I resign?

On Thursday afternoon, I was summoned to Howard Baker's office, where Howard and Jim Baker were present but no one else. The two of them showed me a copy of the statement the president was about to issue as well as a draft of the president's opening statement for the press conference that had been scheduled that evening. The statement to be issued in the president's name was bad enough, for it clearly telegraphed the president's acquiescence to congressional demands that taxes be on the table. I argued that this would dissipate the president's capital on the tax issue even if he ended up not accepting a tax increase. Jim Baker argued strongly that this statement was necessary to obtain congressional agreement to a meeting, that such a meeting was absolutely essential to calm markets, and that we could still oppose a tax increase even if it were on the table. I responded that this arrangement was based on a wholly erroneous premise— namely, that markets would be swayed by whether or not the president agreed to get together with the congressional leadership.

But far more serious for me personally was the draft of the president's opening statement at the press conference, for it indicated that he was directing that negotiations be carried out by his team of negotiators: Jim Baker, his secretary of the Treasury, and Howard Baker, his chief of staff. Pointedly omitted was mention of Jim Miller, his director of OMB. I viewed this not only as a personal affront but as evidence that the moderates had fully captured the president on the issue of taxes or the Speaker had prevailed in his opposition to my participation or both. In what was for me the most tense and depressing meeting of the year, I stated that if my name were not added to the presidential statement, I demanded to speak personally with the president. Both Bakers indicated there would be trouble including me as a formal member of the negotiating team, although they did not identify whom it might trouble.[7]

Of course, omitting me from the negotiating team would please the congressional Democratic leadership. After all, they wanted to deal; I represented an

---

[7] It later became clear that the person I troubled the most was House Speaker Jim Wright.

obstacle to such a deal. But I was convinced that the president was not behind my exclusion from the negotiating team. Sitting there, I was as certain, however, that should the president not support me, I would have no choice but to resign. The matter was not strictly personal; if the president does not feel comfortable including his budget director in negotiations over a budget compromise with Congress, the president needs a new budget director. Moreover, as an institution, OMB cannot be led by a director excluded from budget negotiations. Howard Baker said he would raise my insistence on this matter with the president.

Dispirited, I returned to my office. The fiscal principle President Reagan had held onto most dearly—opposition to a tax increase—was about to be thrown to the wind. Moreover, my personal views on this issue were so adverse to a tax increase, I wondered whether, even with the president's personal support, I could be an effective participant in the negotiations.

At the regularly scheduled 5:00 P.M. meeting with my senior staff, I covered the day's events quickly and discussed several technical matters dealing with the budget. I then excused all but a handful—those whom I had known the longest—and Demaris, who had just arrived from work. I brought the remaining few up to speed and told them I was seriously thinking of resigning and why: my views had been excluded from the president's ears and my effectiveness was in jeopardy. Most responded with great surprise, for they knew of my devotion to President Reagan and my repeated assertions that when I left it would be for personal reasons, not policy differences. Although sympathetic, they argued that if the president included my name in his address that evening, it would represent a substantial victory and evidence that my clout was intact. Several others argued that for me to resign now would harm the president when he really needed me in the upcoming negotiations.

The discussion lasted some thirty minutes, during which the pros and the cons were weighed. The consensus was that, *provided* my name were included in the president's remarks, I should not resign. A few moments later, Howard Baker called and said that my name had, indeed, been inserted in the draft of the president's opening statement.

Although the president's remarks implied that taxes were on the table, the tenor of his responses to specific questions clearly indicated his continued strong objection to any tax increase. This, apparently, contributed to holding further deterioration in the market, for the market closed on Friday where it began Friday morning, at 1,951—296 points below its close of the previous Friday but up 212 points from its close on Black Monday (see figure 7).

7 | The Budget Summit

ON MONDAY, OCTOBER 26, 1987, the president had the "big five" congressional leaders (House Speaker Jim Wright, Majority leaders Bob Byrd and Tom Foley, and Minority leaders Bob Dole and Bob Michel) to the White House for the kickoff session of the budget summit. The president said he wished to avoid a sequester by coming up with a more rational package. He reiterated that "everything is on the table, except Social Security." He also admonished us all to work hard to reach an agreement because "the whole world is looking at us."

Wright and others responded, acknowledging that the stakes were high. All pledged their cooperation and determination to "make this thing work." There were discussions about procedure and logistics. The president and the leaders decided that all the sessions would be held on Capitol Hill, except those directly involving the president (as it turned out, only the opening and closing sessions); these would be held at the White House. The president said his negotiating team would consist of Baker, Baker, Miller, and, when defense issues were discussed, Frank Carlucci, the national security adviser. The congressional team would be balanced—chairs or ranking members from the Budget, Appropriations, Ways and Means/Finance committees, plus one each designated by the majority and minority leaders in each house—sixteen in all. This would keep the total at twenty or below—a manageable number. Finally, it was also decided that the negotiators' role would be to fashion a package to present for the leaders' consideration. Thus, our role as negotiators was to put together a proposal that would not become final until all the leaders (the big five plus the president) endorsed it.

The negotiations begin

The actual negotiating sessions began on Tuesday, October 27, in room 217 of the Capitol amid a flurry of activity. Reporters and photographers were everywhere, shouting questions, angling for the best shots. This did not let up until the end of the sessions nearly four weeks later.

After the press left, we quickly settled down to work. Tom Foley was accepted as chairman of the group by acclamation. A short time later, the staff was asked to leave. (The presence of staff had been disturbing to many of us and had been thoroughly discussed at the meeting with the president; all agreed it was better for staff not to be in the room but on call.) In the actual negotiating sessions, however, there would typically be fourteen or fifteen (of the nineteen or twenty) principals in the room, together with a large staff sometimes numbering more than fifty—an unwieldy arrangement.

At the first session, we discussed spending and revenue baselines. I suggested using the revised Gramm-Rudman-Hollings baseline—the report OMB had published the previous week (October 20).[1] This was accepted. Pete Domenici also suggested we use 1987 actual spending levels as a baseline, and it was agreed that our tables would show both levels to give the conferees a feel for what was being proposed.

The discussion of baselines was important, for they were to become the standard against which all proposals were measured. But there were problems, partly because everyone agreed we wanted to strive for a multiyear agreement with two years being the minimum. An official Gramm-Rudman-Hollings baseline existed for 1988 but not for 1989. An extrapolated 1989 baseline was prepared by OMB staff, but it was not universally accepted and proved to be the source of many differences on the effects of the spending adjustments in subsequent sessions. Also, the 1987 fiscal year had just ended, and even the administration's experts in OMB and Treasury didn't know precisely how much had been spent in each programmatic category. So even this baseline was subject to dispute. All this led to a good deal of disagreement over the effects the various proposals might have on total spending.

From my standpoint as President Reagan's representative, there were advantages in both baselines. The Gramm-Rudman-Hollings baseline put defense budget authority at the $302 billion level. This was more than we anticipated

---

[1] Roughly speaking, the Gramm-Rudman-Hollings baseline is the same as the current services baseline (see discussion in chapter 10).

getting for 1988, but it gave us some leverage in arguing the point. Of course, had President Reagan not been so adamant about increasing spending for defense, I would have disposed with the Gramm-Rudman-Hollings baseline entirely and argued for 1987 spending levels as the appropriate point of departure. The 1987 baseline was also important because both domestic discretionary programs and domestic entitlement spending would go way up under any scenario I thought achievable in the budget talks. Using that baseline would give us leverage in trying to hold such spending within bounds.[2]

During the remainder of that day's session, there were discussions of whether the House would hold up passage of its reconciliation bill (containing new taxes and expansions in entitlement programs) because this would be one of the two major vehicles for carrying out the agreement. Foley indicated that the reconciliation bill would go forward, that this was "not negotiable." As we had anticipated, the Speaker was bound and determined to push this matter and put the administration and congressional Republicans under intense pressure: either agree to the Democrats' terms in the negotiations or accept their solution by having the reconciliation bill rammed down their throats. Foley also indicated that the position of the House Democrats was that the agreement should be a fifty-fifty split between revenue increases and outlay reductions and that the outlay reductions should be split fifty-fifty between domestic spending and defense spending, "in accord with the Gramm-Rudman-Hollings formula."[3] We adjourned to reconvene at 10:15 A.M. the next day.

Early the next morning (Wednesday), the Bakers, several others, and I commenced what would become a morning ritual—meeting in Howard Baker's office to decide on a strategy for the day's session of the budget summit. We agreed that we faced several major problems. First, it would be extremely difficult to obtain cuts in domestic discretionary (that is, appropriated) programs.[4] Second, without substantial cuts in entitlement spending, the domestic program reductions would be paltry. Third, increasing defense spending—much less getting anything like what the president wanted—would be an uphill battle. And fourth, it would be difficult to hold revenue increases within bounds.

Jim Baker hit on the idea of pairing revenue increases with reductions in *domestic* outlays. This had two advantages. First, because the Democrats would

---

[2] See discussion of the current services baseline in chapter 10.

[3] Of course the Gramm-Rudman-Hollings formula contemplated no revenue increase, only across-the-board cuts in spending.

[4] Throughout most of the negotiations, discussions of spending cuts were relative to the Gramm-Rudman-Hollings (that is, current services) baseline—meaning that a program could be cut but spending on it still exceed the previous year's level. Even we in the administration fell into this sloppy habit of imprecision in budget language.

want revenue increases, they might be willing to give up some domestic outlays to get them.[5] Second, the Democrats, being resistant to domestic cuts, would therefore hold the revenue figure within bounds. It was a great idea if it would work. (In the end, the formula didn't hold, but we were able to make progress by putting forth this argument.)

I urged we pursue *a spending freeze* (limiting total spending by major categories to 1987 levels), saying this would be easy to explain and had quite a following.[6] Moreover, if it were a freeze on budget authority, defense would make out reasonably well—in fact, better than we would likely get through the appropriations process. We agreed on this as part of the opening strategy.

When the budget session opened, Jim Baker put on the table a freeze in defense and domestic discretionary budget authority; for every one dollar in *further* domestic outlay cuts (including entitlements), we would match them with a dollar increase in tax revenues. He also suggested we attempt to go beyond the amount needed to avoid a sequester "in order to impress markets"; this could include onetime revenue such as asset sales.

After a diversion in which the House Republicans raised objections to the House leadership's proceeding with the reconciliation bill, we returned to the issue of specific savings. To my surprise, there was wide consensus that we should address the outlay reductions before the revenue increases. During the course of the morning's discussion, I raised the idea of a modified freeze on entitlements—forgoing all cost-of-living adjustments (COLAs) except those on Social Security.[7] By our figures, such a freeze would restrain spending increases and therefore save $2.0 billion in Medicare, $1.8 billion in Medicaid, $2.4 billion in retirement programs, and $0.1 billion elsewhere for a total $6.2 billion. That proposal received some attention, but there was a great deal of grousing about harming retirees while letting those on Social Security go scot-free. Also, the Democrats protested this would not comport with their fifty-fifty outlay reduction principle.

In deference to the president's aversion to talking about taxes, we quickly hit on revenue symbols. *R-one* (R_1) meant recurring revenue on the receipts side, or taxes to the Democrats; R_2 was user fees, or what the president called "fees for

---

[5] Even this early in the negotiations, given my reading of the congressional negotiators and my colleagues, and in view of the president's desire to get an agreement, I had abandoned all hope of securing a deal without new taxes. My objective was to make the increase as small as possible.

[6] Such a scheme had been advanced by the organization of which I am now chairman, Citizens for a Sound Economy.

[7] I am not a fan of restraining COLAs, for it smacks of the federal government's abrogating a contract. However, it apeared this device might be the only one capable of limiting increases in entitlement spending.

services"; and R_3 stood for asset sales, such as the Naval Petroleum Reserve or loan portfolios.[8] As I pointed out, if the Democrats would accept R_3s as revenues, then we could have a pairing of increased revenues and outlay reductions according to our principles as well as theirs. For example, suppose you had $5 billion increments in each of the following areas: R_1, R_2, R_3, defense, domestic discretionary, and entitlements. Our recurring revenues (R_1 plus R_2) would, indeed, match domestic cuts (domestic discretionary and entitlements);[9] also, total revenues (including R_3) would equal total outlay reductions (including defense).

The Democrats found this formulation interesting but unacceptable. They wanted fifty-fifty cuts in domestic and defense programs, not two-thirds domestic, one-third defense; and they wanted much more in the way of hard revenues—R_1.

On Thursday, October 29, the negotiators met again in the ornate Senate room that had once been Lyndon Johnson's Capitol office. Discussions arose over baselines, in particular the budget authority/budget outlay mismatch in the defense account. As I had described in the first session on Tuesday, the defense account in the Gramm-Rudman-Hollings baseline contained a substantial shortfall in outlays compared with the amount of budget authority. This had to be fixed.[10] But on Thursday, it was plain that the negotiators had been talking past one another; except for the members of the appropriations committees and a few from the budget committees, the negotiators had little understanding of what was being discussed or its ramifications. After all, this was pretty technical stuff even for most experts.

On Friday, October 30, our chairman, Tom Foley, suggested that a group of budget committee representatives (Lawton Chiles [D., Fla.], Pete Domenici, Bill Gray, and Del Latta [R., Ohio]) convene to put together a specific outlay-reduction proposal for us to consider. Lloyd Bentsen (D., Tex.) then suggested

---

[8] The Naval Petroleum Reserve consists of land in Wyoming and California that is leased to companies from which they extract crude oil; even producing at full capacity, these fields would provide only a small fraction of the navy's needs. Also, as a product of its various loan programs—to farmers, students, businesses, and so forth—the federal government holds large portfolios of loan assets (promises to pay) that can and should be sold to the private sector (see discussion in chapter 10).

[9] By then, the discussion had evolved into matching *total* domestic outlay reductions with revenue increases (instead of reductions below a freeze as we had proposed initially).

[10] Gramm-Rudman-Hollings required the baseline to be constructed keeping the ratio of budget authority to budget outlays constant. But with the bringing on-line of new weapons systems (previously paid for), a larger and larger fraction of the defense budget went for personnel, operations, and maintenance. Thus, to forecast spending accurately, the ratio of outlays to budget authority had to be raised every year.

that representatives of the Ways and Means/Finance committees (Dan Rosten-kowski [D., Ill.], John Duncan [R., Tenn.], Lloyd Bentsen, and Bob Packwood [R., Oreg.]) meet in another room to work on a revenue proposal. Jim Baker then met with the revenue group, while I stayed with the outlay group.

Pete Domenici tabled a "soft freeze" in spending—no change in budget authority but adding money for a pay increase and retirement COLAs for federal retirees, in essence, a 2 percent increase in total spending. He also suggested limiting nonmeans-tested entitlement programs[11] to a 2 percent increase, includ-ing Social Security. Domenici's plan became known as the "2 percent solution," with apologies to Sir Arthur Conan Doyle.

Many in the room spoke strongly about the need for some limit on Social Security. Of particular concern was the idea of restraining non–Social Security COLAs, while Social Security recipients got an estimated 4.2 percent increase. Some of the negotiators were not at all skittish about discussing Social Security; some who were cast their eyes around the room at various staff members, won-dering whether word of this heresy would get out. Foley indicated that, "for the record," Social Security was off the table.

Around 5:00, Senate majority leader Bob Byrd, as well as House Speaker Jim Wright, came to the meeting, and shortly thereafter the staff was excused. Although both men were cordial, it quickly became apparent that they had come on a precise mission. That mission was to inform the White House negotiators that if the president did not agree to revenue increases in excess of $8 billion (which Jim Baker had been hinting was an absolute maximum), they and the Republican leaders would go down and alert the president to the "reality" of the situation. Moreover, the Speaker said he would not address the issue of Social Security at that time. After indicating his understanding that we were up against a resolute president, he looked over and said to Jim Baker, "Jim, you are doing your best, but your best is not good enough." In other words, Baker would have to persuade the president to increase taxes—by a lot.

Throughout that first week, the negotiators monitored what was happening to the stock market. Later, Howard Baker was to say that when the market went up, the negotiators became lackadaisical, but when the market went down, they got serious (see figure 8). Although this was an overstatement, there did tend to be a relationship between what the market was doing and the intensity of the negotiations. This effect was accentuated on Friday by reports that the leading economic indicators had fallen the previous month by 0.1 percent and that the sale of new one-family houses had declined by 5.2 percent in September.

---

[11] As described in the Appendix, means-tested entitlement programs are those where eligibility is determined by income and/or wealth. In other words, if you have the means, you don't qualify.

Figure 8:   Dow-Jones, Month of Negotiations

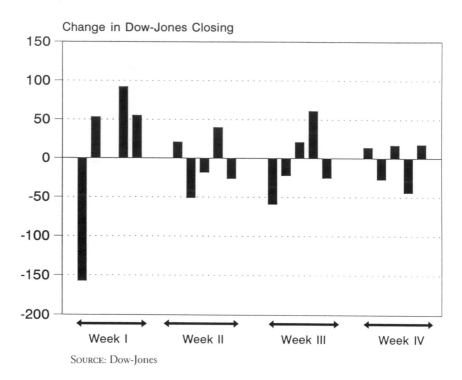

Change in Dow-Jones Closing

SOURCE: Dow-Jones

The negotiators agreed to meet the next day, Saturday. Friday evening I put together the first of a number of tables showing deficit-reduction possibilities. By our estimates, a soft freeze, including a 2.0 percent restraint on nonmeans-tested COLAs, would form the backbone of a package reducing the deficit some $30.2 billion from the Gramm-Rudman-Hollings baseline in 1988 and $50.9 billion in 1989.[12] Included in the package (for 1988) were $10.0 billion in new receipts (taxes) and user fees and $4.9 billion in asset sales for a total of $14.9 billion in new revenue. Cuts in discretionary outlays (for 1988) were $3.4 billion for defense, $0.4 billion for international affairs, and $2.4 billion for domestic programs. The package also included $4.5 billion in savings from restraints on entitlement COLAs and $3.4 billion in other entitlement savings. This gave a

---

[12] In this package, total spending would go up but not as much as it would if spending were left on automatic pilot (in other words, reached current services levels). Receipts to the government would go up *more* than if left on automatic pilot.

total outlay savings of $14.1 billion, which, added to the revenues and reflecting a reduction in debt service expense of $1.2 billion, gave us the $30.2 billion deficit-reduction figure. The meeting on Saturday quickly proved less than satisfactory and was adjourned at lunchtime.

Week two

On Monday morning, November 2, we (Baker/Baker/Miller) met with President Reagan in the Oval Office. The president was not in a good mood. An op-ed by Senator Patrick Moynihan (D., N.Y.) had appeared in the Sunday *New York Times*[13] that seemed to blame the president for the market collapse and accused him of "deliberately misleading" the public.

The president was also concerned about polls showing that an increasing number of people believed the president was responsible for the deficit and in fact had tried to conceal the deficit from them. He said he was considering a speech explaining the cause of the deficit and how taxes would exacerbate the problem.

Howard Baker reported that there had been some progress in the budget summit but that until Friday there had been no firm proposals. But on Friday, several members had proposed a 2 percent cap on COLAs, including Social Security. The president all but exploded. "Social Security has nothing to do with the deficit; it's self-financing," he exclaimed. Howard explained some advantages of the proposal that had been discussed but stressed that there was no assurance whatever the Democrats would actually deliver votes on any proposal that tampered with Social Security and that any hint of administration acceptance of such a proposal might box us in politically. There was discussion all around. The president indicated reluctance to go along with a Social Security cap of any kind, but he agreed to match dollar for dollar outlay cuts in domestic discretionary spending with revenue increases, up to a maximum of $11 billion.

We then left for the budget negotiations on the Hill, this time in the House Ways and Means Committee room on the House side of the Capitol.[14] The discussion was mainly about the COLA plan and its hit on Social Security. Someone produced a letter from one of the veterans' organizations that said they would be willing to accept a COLA freeze in veterans' retirement benefits but only if it were matched by a freeze in Social Security COLAs. There was general

---

[13] Daniel P. Moynihan, "How Reagan Created the Crash," *New York Times*, November 1, 1987, p. E25.

[14] During weeks one and three of the budget summit, the negotiations were held on the Senate side of the Capitol; during weeks two and four, they were held on the House side.

agreement around the table that we couldn't touch other COLAs and leave Social Security unscathed.

During the afternoon session, to almost everyone's surprise, Jim Baker agreed to a $10.7 billion R_1 (tax) package, *provided* it were matched by domestic outlay reductions. But the Democrats balked. Tom Foley said we must have some "equity" in the revenues, the first mention of what would become a recurring theme. Yes, they would like to control entitlement spending, but, no, they would not do so unless we sweetened the deal not only with additional taxes but with *certain types of taxes*—specifically, "soak the rich" taxes. The Democrats suggested holding off the reduction in the higher marginal tax rate coming out of the 1986 tax reform package and indexing the tax code a maximum of 2 percent a year, consistent with the so-called 2 percent solution. I indicated that both ideas were simply "nonstarters"; the president would veto any package containing these provisions.

On Tuesday, November 3, in our morning meeting at the White House, we negotiators discussed the difficult situation in which we found ourselves. "The world is expecting an agreement," said Jim Baker. But it was also plain that the Democrats were not willing to give us much in the way of outlay reductions and that they wanted a big tax increase and certain types of taxes at that. What was even more troubling was the reluctance of the congressional negotiators to agree on some kind of enforcement mechanism. Despite the fact that from day one Howard Baker had been insisting that any agreement be "fair and enforceable," every time we brought up developing some kind of mechanism to enforce an agreement, the Democrats would change the subject.

The night before, I had written down my own minimal enforcement proposal, namely, that Congress put into law the budget figures we eventually accepted for 1988 and 1989. The Bakers liked that idea. We agreed also that (a) the House and Senate reconciliation bills would have to wipe away all the expansions in entitlements and start over,[15] (b) the defense budget authority/outlay problem would have to be fixed, and (c) the reconciliation (tax and entitlement) and appropriations bills would have to be presented to the president at the same time.[16] When I presented these proposals to the budget negotiators, they were roundly criticized. When I suggested that certain budget reform measures be included, such as a vote on a balanced budget amendment, a vote on a

---

[15] The reconciliation bills in both Houses included program expansions that would increase total spending. Now the Democrats wanted to pocket these increases and discuss reductions from this new, higher baseline, not the Gramm-Rudman-Hollings baseline.

[16] The president obviously didn't want to sign a tax increase and not get the (discretionary) spending reductions. On the other hand, the Democrats didn't want to risk enacting outlay reductions and then have the president veto the tax increase.

line-item veto, or a vote on enhanced rescission authority,[17] the Democrats changed the subject. Increasingly, so it seemed, we were about to be taken down the primrose path of agreeing to revenue increases that were real, to defense cuts that were real, but to domestic cuts that might conceivably be obtained in the sweet by-and-by.

At the morning meeting of Wednesday, November 4, for the first time we in the administration began to explore the possibility that the budget negotiations would end without an agreement. There seemed to be too wide a gulf between what the Democrats wanted—taxes, defense cuts but no real reductions in domestic spending—and what we wanted, just the opposite. We decided, however, to go the extra mile. No one could say we failed to do our duty.

At the negotiating session, we reviewed the various proposals again. During much of this time, Tom Foley kept things going by sheer strength of will and by repeatedly going over the proposals and what had been tentatively agreed on. Some House appropriators argued that even the 2 percent solution—with its $2.4 billion cut in domestic discretionary spending—would require too great a reduction from what the House had already passed.[18]

At noon, the three of us from the administration met in Bob Dole's office with several key Republican senators. All seemed to like the 2 percent solution, but some voiced reservations about generating support from their colleagues (Republicans as a rule don't like taxes). Dole suggested that we needed some kind of bold plan. Concerns were expressed about the economy, and Howard Baker reported that Dick Wirthlin's[19] latest poll showed that 92 percent of the public preferred some sort of bipartisan solution to 7 percent who preferred no solution. Later, we met in Bob Michel's office, where the discussion was more contentious; the House Republicans did not want any new taxes or—heaven help us!—any cut in Social Security.

On Thursday morning, November 5, we met with President Reagan and explained the benefits of the packages being considered. After some discussion about Social Security and how cuts in entitlement programs would hinge on some restraint of Social Security, the president reluctantly agreed to consider such a package, *provided* it would be bipartisan—that the whole congressional leadership, perhaps even including the party chairmen, endorse it publicly and

---

[17] Under enhanced rescission authority—an idea being championed by then Senator Dan Quayle—Congress would be forced to *vote* on the rescission proposals it typically ignored (see the Appendix and discussion in chapter 10).

[18] Before the onset of negotiations, the House had already passed domestic discretionary spending measures at levels exceeding the Gramm-Rudman-Hollings baseline.

[19] Richard Wirthlin, founder of the Wirthlin Group of McLean, Virginia, served as President Reagan's chief pollster.

at the same time. The president also indicated that he wanted to approve all specific revenue increases. Jim Baker suggested particular measures that were not included in his budget but that might be worth accepting, such as collecting diesel fuel taxes at the source rather than at the retail level. The president said, "I can support that on efficiency grounds." But the president became particularly angry at the Democrats. He speculated that they wanted the budget negotiations to fail because they wanted a recession. He said to us, "Tell them that if this goes down, I'll go to the American people and claim they did this in order to force a recession in hopes of winning the 1988 election."

The budget conference opened that morning with a feeling that perhaps some kind of breakthrough was imminent. Chairman Foley went through the variations of the latest proposal, dubbed the "Chiles/Gray" plan because it was conceived by Lawton Chiles and Bill Gray. Pete Domenici then volunteered to table a variation of Chiles/Gray but in private, so we cleared the room of staff. We then reviewed the Domenici plan, which basically was a more ambitious version containing more taxes and more cuts in entitlement programs. But toward the end of the afternoon session the Democrats raised the ante. They wanted tax equity; they felt there were too many cuts in domestic programs, too little in new revenue, and too much for defense. They argued that in the current configuration they couldn't sell the package to their constituents (that is, other Democrats in Congress).

Bennett Johnston and Lloyd Bentsen argued for an oil import fee. Others brought up higher marginal tax rates on income or a 2 percent cap on tax indexing. I got the feeling the Democrats were not really serious. Every time it looked like we were close to a deal, they upped the ante. And just to cap things off, Speaker Wright, at his daily press conference, suggested a spending cut that would take $11.2 billion out of defense and international affairs but only $0.8 billion out of domestic spending.

Things were really bogged down now, so Bob Dole and Bob Michel approached the president for a meeting. "Either we move forward or we get out," one said. The next morning, Friday, November 6, the GOP leadership and the GOP negotiators came to the White House. But first, Howard Baker, Jim Baker, and I met with the president. We agreed it would be useful to have a deal but not at any cost.

We then joined the GOP representatives in the cabinet room. Bob Dole noted that we had been meeting for ten days and should be showing some momentum but that the Democrats wanted to raise taxes and had even discussed cutting Social Security. "The Republicans have the high ground," he said. The president then reiterated his view that he was not sure the Democrats wanted to avoid a recession. Bob Michel opined that we needed to get back to basics. "We should point out that what the Democrats are talking about is a big spending increase over last year's level," he said. "Why not just a freeze? Or maybe freeze outlays for six months and then have a 2 percent increase? The Democrats are stringing us out; they may not even want an agreement."

Howard Baker suggested that it was time for the Republican leadership to table a specific proposal. He noted that the 2 percent solution was on the table but that the Democrats were backpedaling; if we wanted to get an agreement we needed to table something quickly.

Jim Baker cautioned that getting an agreement would be good but that the Democrats were demanding a high price, not only in terms of revenue levels but in specifics: soak-the-rich taxes, oil import fees, and so forth. The president noted that what the Democrats appeared to want is what they have always wanted: increased taxes. He said that if Republicans went for a Social Security cut and more taxes, the Democrats would have a field day in the 1988 campaign. He also argued that tax rate increases *reduce* total revenue, not increase it.

Howard Baker observed that the Democrats professed devotion to some kind of COLA restraint but that they kept raising the ante. He expressed concern that the Democrats might be setting us up. He wasn't even sure the Democrats wanted to avoid a sequester: "What they may do is send the president a bill with too much in taxes and have the president veto it." Bob Dole then suggested we smoke the Democrats out: "We need to strike today."

The discussion then turned to what we might propose. I suggested a freeze or some variation on that theme. Bob Michel then proposed a six-month freeze followed by a 2 percent increase. Dole endorsed the freeze idea, and we settled on Michel's plan. The president suggested we promptly lay our package on the table and let the Democrats come back to us.

I rushed back to the office to prepare the numbers on Michel's semifreeze. With lots of help, I was able to get the table of numbers put together, typed, and to Capitol Hill in time for the beginning of the session. Just before the press was allowed in, a House aide began handing out copies of the Michel plan to the principals. After the press departed, Tom Foley exclaimed in disgust that he understood the press now had copies of the Michel plan. He also expressed his grave concern that now we had a "Republican plan," whereas before there had been general agreement that plans would be nonpartisan.[20] The rest of the day was taken up with discussions of the Michel plan: how the numbers were arrived at and how it would work.

We decided not to meet the following day (Saturday). Jim Baker went to Texas to visit his sick mother. Howard Baker left for Tennessee. And the Millers went to the cabin to get a broader perspective on things and to nurse my increasingly bad and debilitating cold.

---

[20] Of course, newspapers had been widely reporting Chiles/Gray as the "Democratic leadership proposal."

Week three

On Monday, November 9, the Democrats responded to the Michel plan. They would pocket the defense cuts, thank you very much, as well as the revenue increases, even though they thought these were short of what was necessary. However, they felt they must have more time to put together their specific response and so suggested we adjourn the meeting.

After returning to my office, I was discouraged and becoming increasingly concerned that, whether by premeditation or accident, the Democrats might trap the president into a political "worst-case scenario." First, the president would be seen as having caved in on his resolve never to increase taxes, thus taking away the Republicans' ability to use this theme as a rallying cry for the 1988 elections. Second, the president would be seen as having been willing to put Social Security on the table, thus providing the Democrats with the same issue with which they soundly beat the Republicans in 1982. And finally, the president would be blamed for breaking off the negotiations, and any adversity experienced by the economy, whatever the reasons, would be blamed on the president.

On Tuesday, November 10, the Democrats laid on the table what became known as the Foley/Gray plan: $12.0 billion in taxes, user fees, and increased Internal Revenue Service (IRS) enforcement (that is, more collections of taxes due) to get a total of $14.9 billion in revenues. The outlay reductions called for a $5.4 billion cut in defense, a $2.4 billion cut in domestic discretionary programs, and a $3.5 billion cut in entitlement programs. So, in real outlay reductions (including defense), there would be $11.3 billion,[21] as contrasted with $12.0 billion in new revenue. Our response to Foley/Gray was halting, and we sought clarification. In retrospect, we should have asked for a recess to evaluate their plan. Instead, the seriousness of our response emboldened the Democrats. (According to later reports, they considered Foley/Gray a strategic ploy; our taking it seriously caused them to ask for even more.)

On Wednesday, November 11 (Veterans Day), there was a giant snowstorm, which left over a foot of snow—a record for Washington in November. However, inside the meeting room there was an air of anticipation.

Before the meeting, Jim Baker, Howard Baker, and I discussed the possibilities. Jim Baker was anxious to close a deal. He and I discussed the latest version of Foley/Gray—a solution that, from the president's standpoint, I felt was only

---

[21] This was in contrast to a plan we had discussed in Howard Baker's office earlier that day—$4 billion in each area: defense, domestic discretionary, and entitlements.

marginally better than a sequester. But we agreed that to make progress we would have to get staff removed from the room (to avoid posturing on the part of the principals).

Shortly after the budget session began, I handed a note to Tom Foley, suggesting that if we really wanted to get serious we should ask staff to leave. After a short time interval, Foley announced, "There has been a request for staff to leave." Danny Rostenkowski then queried forcefully, "Who asked staff to leave?" I could well have remained mum and Foley would have covered by saying it was an anonymous request, but instead I said, "I did." "Why?" asked Rostenkowski. I retorted that it had little to do with staff, per se, but that I had observed that progress was much faster when staff were out of the room and that if we were really serious about reaching an agreement, we should speed up the process. Staff were then excused, but I knew I would be in for some serious criticism because staff understandably prefer to be in on things.

After the staff members left, Bob Packwood tabled what became known as the Packwood/Gray plan. It contained $11.5 billion in revenue increases and $10.4 billion in outlay reductions. Together with additional IRS enforcement, asset sales, and savings on debt service, this proposal constituted a total of $31.3 billion in deficit reduction (for 1988). We discussed Packwood/Gray for the rest of the day. That evening, somewhat tongue in cheek, I wrote up a devil's advocate position on the Packwood/Gray plan: "Mr. President, we have good news and bad news. The good news is that we've cut $2.0 billion from domestic discretionary spending and we've cut $2.8 billion from entitlement programs. The bad news is that we've taken a $5.0 billion hit on defense, a $0.6 billion hit on international programs,[22] and a tax increase of $9.0 billion."

The next morning (Thursday, November 12), we met in Howard Baker's office. Jim Baker maintained that the Packwood/Gray package wasn't good but that we ought to support it because "markets demand it." I demurred. Jim Baker then took up a pen and racked up the "pain versus gain" provisions of Packwood/Gray and came up with close to a tie. He said that because "markets demand an agreement," we ought to support it even though the rack-up came out a tie. I disagreed. Jim Baker, now highly agitated, said, "We either make a deal or we don't; make up your mind." I replied that we shouldn't go for just any deal. The situation got testy.

At 9:15, we went in to see the president. Howard Baker summarized, saying "Carlucci can live with the Packwood/Gray DOD [Department of Defense] number." He then turned to Jim Baker, who said that Packwood/Gray was a bad

---

[22] The president was almost as animated about protecting international programs (particularly foreign aid) as he was about protecting defense.

deal but that the president's leadership was at stake and "markets demand it."
Then I proceeded to make a short presentation:

> The first thing, Mr. President, is that I work for you and will be a good soldier
> in carrying out your decisions. But I do believe I owe it to you to give you an
> honest appraisal of the situation.
> The cut in defense at $5.0 billion is excessive; the cut in international affairs
> at $0.6 billion is problematical; but the cuts in domestic programs are paltry—
> only $2.0 billion in domestic discretionary spending and $2.8 billion in entitle-
> ments. Also, the tax increase at $9.0 billion is far above the receipts numbers
> in your own budget. Moreover, there is no enforcement mechanism yet in place.
> None of your budget process reforms are part of the package. While I do not
> believe these problems are insurmountable, on the merits I would advise your
> not accepting this package.
> Moreover, with respect to the broader question of whether or not we get an
> agreement, I concur that everything else equal it would be better to get an
> agreement than to have the negotiations break up. But I question at what price.
> Basically, I have a fundamental difference with my two colleagues over the likely
> effect of having these negotiations fall through—that is, I do not believe that
> markets would respond negatively in the long run to lack of an agreement.
> Finally, with respect to where we go from here, I propose that we keep the
> discussions going, that we press for an enforcement mechanism, that we press
> for a better deal, and that we press for evidence that the Democrats want to deal,
> rather than just string us along. But I propose that we prepare for failure—
> minimizing the blame that would accrue to you, Mr. President, and gird our
> loins for the rough and tumble of negotiations over a continuing resolution and
> a reconciliation bill.

During my presentation, the president interrupted me several times to con-
demn Congress for cutting defense and not cutting domestic spending. After my
presentation, Frank Carlucci said that he would "make do" with any number he
was given for defense but that he believed the defense number in Packwood/Gray
was *not* sufficient. The president then leaned over to me and said sternly, "This
deal is not good enough; we must get more for defense and greater cuts in domestic
spending." We had our marching orders.

The three of us then went to the Capitol. Howard Baker reported that the
president believed we should get more for defense and greater cuts in domestic
spending. Leon Panetta then tabled a three-month freeze in nonmeans-tested
COLAs and the federal pay increase. I was slipped a note to call my office; one
of my assistants reported that someone from the *Washington Times* had phoned,
saying that spokesmen for both Chiles and Gray were calling reporters saying we
had had a deal the day before but that now things had broken down because I
was being a "hardass on defense."

At 12:30, we met with twenty or so Republican senators in Bob Dole's office.

Jim Baker laid out the Packwood/Gray plan. The first senator[23] said it looked reasonably good. Senator number two said that it had some advantages for defense but that a sequester wouldn't be bad either; however, we had only a short time to put something together, so time was of the essence. Senator number three complained about the defense number but said we had to move forward. Senator four said that this was the "most minimalist package" he could imagine and that if we didn't get an enforcement package, he would vote against it. He also said the Republicans should be writing the tax package, not the Democrats. If all this did come together, however, he would vote for it.

Senator five said we must all support what came out of the group: "markets depend on it." Senator six said there was a lot at stake for the economy. A sequester would send a signal that the government doesn't work. If we could get a two-year package with real savings, then it would be worth it. Senator seven said that he agreed with Senators five and six and furthermore thought we must have COLA restraints. Senator eight raised a question about user fees. Senator nine said he was disappointed, mainly about the tax numbers. He thought a sequester would be better—at least we'd get real cuts in domestic spending. Senator ten said that this was a marginally better package than sequestration but that the message sent to the country would be terrible either way. Senator eleven noted our success the previous year: outlays had gone up by only 1 percent; however, he agreed with Senator ten that we needed to go along with the deal.

Senator twelve noted that the package would be hard to sell: too much tax increase and too little cut in domestic spending. Senator thirteen asked, why give federal workers any increase while farmers take cuts? Senator fourteen observed that the negotiators had worked hard and they should be supported. Senator fifteen said that he would swallow anything we came up with but that we were foolish to be driven by the current squabble—the real challenge was in the greater cuts the negotiators were apparently unwilling to make. Senator four pointed out that financial markets were not likely to be fooled by what we accomplished: "If they are in the market, they are fairly well-off, and these people are not stupid."

At 2:00, the negotiators reconvened. I told Bill Gray about the report that I was being a "hardass on defense"; he denied any knowledge of such telephone calls. Later, after being handed a note by a staffer, Pete Domenici announced that one of the Democratic negotiators had just told reporters that the White House had torpedoed the talks. Tom Foley responded, "I can't control my people." At that moment, the negotiations appeared to be at the point of breaking up for good. Indeed, this was the low point of the whole process. After a quick break, Lawton Chiles tabled yet another proposal that was a variation on previous themes

---

[23] Because of the candid, freewheeling nature of this discussion, I will not reveal the names of the senators.

but got us back to business. Both Tom Foley and Howard Baker responded to the increasing excitement among reporters (who had the story that the talks were breaking up) to the effect that the negotiators continued to make progress.

The next morning (Friday, November 13), the newspapers contained stories indicating there had been rancor among the negotiators along with charges and countercharges. The principal theme was that the White House had torpedoed the negotiations. (Presumably, the chief torpedo was none other than yours truly.)

Chairman Tom Foley opened the session by suggesting we "set aside fifteen minutes for mutual recriminations." There was prolonged silence and then some chuckling. Having no takers, he then proceeded with the business at hand. Rather than going into the Chiles proposal of the previous day, Foley went directly to a proposal we had dismissed before: $5.0 billion in defense cuts, $10 billion in new revenues, $5 billion in entitlement cuts, and so forth. Jamie Whitten, chairman of the House Appropriations Committee, interrupted, "Where did you get those numbers?" And then he proceeded to inform the group that "members of the Appropriations Committee are the only ones with a responsibility to determine discretionary spending." It was an ample opportunity for us to walk out because he was saying that unless we agreed on a package, there was no assurance we would get the cuts in domestic spending or the full funding of defense (whatever levels those might be). This was particularly troubling, and as a result I increased my resolve to get an enforcement mechanism of *some* kind before signing on the dotted line.

At lunch we broke up—oddly enough, with considerably more optimism than the day before. In fact, having weathered the storm the previous day, the negotiators seemed resigned to the fact that a deal would be forthcoming along the lines of the option presently being discussed. In the afternoon, on behalf of the administration, I reiterated the need for enforceable savings. Lloyd Bentsen and Dan Rostenkowski opposed dropping out the reconciliation add-ons, though Bentsen appeared ready to compromise. The staff was instructed to explore the pricing of reconciliation options, especially the Medicare and pay restraint alternatives.

Week four

On Monday, November 16, Chairman Foley opened the session by noting that under current law a sequester was about to be ordered (on November 20). He noted the imperative of our reaching an agreement but indicated that he didn't think Congress, at least the House, could go along with a freeze in COLAs. I presented our assessment of the effects of the various pay options, and, despite Foley's assertion, there seemed to be a great interest in freezing the COLAs for three months and then rebasing certain entitlement programs for 1989. Lawton

Chiles announced that Claude Pepper would be holding a press conference that morning, presumably to oppose any limit on Social Security COLAs.

We returned from lunch to find that staff members had rejoined the group, prompting various elected officials to engage in a great deal of posturing. Bob Packwood, Leon Panetta, and Bill Gray proposed a new compromise, which we then went through. This plan, I noted, contained a substantial increase in domestic discretionary spending from the 1987 level and a further decrease in defense spending from the Gramm-Rudman-Hollings baseline. After considerable debate, Bennett Johnston suggested that we go back to Friday's plan. Foley complained that the administration hadn't offered anything except the president's original budget, that congressional negotiators kept proposing various items and the administration kept resisting them.

After breaking up, the Bakers and I met in the vice-president's office just off the Senate lobby with the Republican negotiators. We decided to accept the Democrats' "offer," provided they agreed to no more than a $4.8 billion cut for defense. But we also agreed with Trent Lott that we find entitlement cuts other than COLA freezes.

The next morning (Tuesday, November 17), we breakfasted at the invitation of Majority leader Bob Byrd in his office. Attending were the big five leaders, plus Baker/Baker/Miller. The notion of tampering with COLAs was generally disparaged. Jim Wright again raised his demand that we have a "balanced" package—hitting high-income earners with what I would characterize as punitive tax increases. Byrd stated that he couldn't pass a revenue package without "equitable" taxes because he needed sixty votes in the Senate (to end any filibuster). There was also a discussion about some kind of resolution to avoid the sequester, scheduled to be implemented on that Friday, November 20. Aside from the need to avoid a sequester, there was the feeling it would be good to send a signal that the negotiators were close to an agreement.

During the morning session we went over all the old territory. But after lunch, we discussed entitlements in great depth. In fact, we spent *five hours* trying to find $1 billion in additional entitlement savings, to be matched by an additional $1 billion in revenue. I laid an administration paper on the table that called for modest revenue increases matched by real reductions in domestic outlays. We debated the defense numbers and talked at length about various dimensions of the proposals on the table. Feeling increasing pressure to put things on the table,[24] we went over into an evening session; before it adjourned at 8:30, we agreed to put the staffs together to draft up some kind of enforcement mechanism—*finally!*

On Wednesday, November 18, we White House negotiators had another

---

[24] At the beginning of the morning session, at each principal's place was a large button that read Real Men Lay It on the Table.

session with the president. The mood was generally upbeat, and he seemed reasonably happy with what appeared to be shaping up. I was late to a session on Capitol Hill devoted to enforcement alternatives, but I found that Tim Muris of OMB and the congressional staff had drafted something that could be used as a starting point.

At the beginning of the formal session, we engaged in a titanic struggle over whether the revenue package provisionally agreed to would be gross or net—that is, whether additional taxes already approved by the Ways and Means/Finance committees would be pocketed or whether the baseline would be Gramm-Rudman-Hollings. Jamie Whitten again said we should not assume the appropriations committees would appropriate the amounts we might agree on for defense. Bentsen and Foley both interjected that we must depend a great deal on faith. I made the point that the president would never say yes to a proposed deal, unless he were assured the deal would be lived up to. Like a skunk at a picnic, I pressed this point over and over.

About 3:30, Howard Baker whispered to me that he wanted to take Bob Michel and Bob Dole down to meet with the president to discuss the situation and suggested that I remain to keep the negotiations going. (The situation on the Republican side was getting serious. That morning the House Republicans had voted ninety-three to four against any deal with the Democrats, and the day before the Senate Republicans had voted thirty-one to six against accepting the current proposal. Republican opposition to the deal was strong and building.)[25] Jim Baker also went down to meet with the president. Before the session on the Hill ended, Tom Foley asked if the group could come up with a few more outlay reductions to be matched by revenue increases "in order to give Jim Miller greater assurance that we would be able to avoid a sequester."[26] Despite our looking for additional savings, we had no luck and adjourned at 5:25 to reconvene the following morning.

On Thursday morning, November 19, the White House negotiators again met in Howard Baker's office. Jim Baker said he was now convinced the Democrats would not give the administration assurances that the deal would be enforced and therefore suggested we begin work on a backup strategy. Accordingly, he had drafted a statement for the president saying that he (the president) would be willing to go the extra mile but that the Democrats wouldn't commit; therefore, he was

[25] In fact, Dole had opened up the morning session by noting that Jack Kemp had already run a TV advertisement in New Hampshire showing Dole at the budget conference "raising taxes." Someone said, humorously, "let the record show that each time taxes came up, Senator Dole said no."

[26] After all, as budget director, I would be making the determination under Gramm-Rudman-Hollings whether congressional action had been sufficient to avoid a sequester.

letting the sequester go into effect. Furthermore, according to Jim Baker's plan, the president would be willing to offer an additional $7 billion to $8 billion in taxes to emphasize his determination to lower the deficit. Howard Baker concurred in this approach. Frank Carlucci raised the problem of defense spending: how do we deal with the devastation in defense accounts? I asked why take a sequester and then give away taxes *without* getting extra money for defense? Jim Baker suggested we do that with a supplemental request. But, I asked, how would we pay for a supplemental if we've already given away the "president's taxes"? Nevertheless, I tended to prefer this approach to accepting the proposal without assurance of enforcement, which was as it now stood. We all agreed that a leak of this position would be *disastrous* and that we should continue the negotiations just in case the Democrats came around.

We then met with the president. Jim Baker sat next to the president and discussed his proposal (the president read the draft text). But first, the president railed against the congressional Iran-*contra* report that had been released the previous day. He complained that the papers were calling him a cheat and a liar and that the committee members had based their work not on what the witnesses had said but on their own previously held opinions. "Heck, I was the one that made all this possible by announcing it all publicly," said the president. "They criticize Ed Meese, but he's the one who found the memo."

Then we discussed Jim Baker's proposal. The president immediately picked up on the lack of protection for defense. Jim agreed this must be added; Carlucci was also concerned. I cautioned against going overboard on any subsequent tax offer. I also pointed out the lack of an enforcement mechanism and said that I would recommend against the deal without a good enforcement package: "You've been had before, Mr. President, and I don't want to have any part in your being had again." We also discussed the difficulty of getting the Republicans to go along with the package. The president then volunteered to address the House Republicans, but we advised against it.

The negotiators reconvened at 10:00 A.M. and, after the photographers left, got started at 10:30.[27] Right off, Bob Packwood reported that the Senate Republicans had voted overwhelmingly against the package. Someone else noted a similar vote by the Republicans in the House. The Democrats responded by saying the Republicans would be responsible for any failure of the negotiations. Handing messages around, I expressed great consternation to my White House colleagues, pointing out that the Republicans were falling into the Democrats'

---

[27] Sil Conte brought along a crystal ball that, when you read it closely, said "it's a joke." He told everyone around the table to ask the crystal ball: "What do you think of the deal?" There was great levity in the room. When the reporters and photographers were allowed into the room, I took out my camera and took photographs of the photographers.

trap. The president would be hard-pressed to blame the Democrats should there be a breakup; instead, all would be blamed on the Republicans. We discussed more details of the various proposals and then broke for a quick lunch in the Senate dining room, after which we went over to the Cannon House office building for a stormy session with House Republicans. Jim Baker summarized the situation, Howard Baker spoke, and then I spoke and responded to questions. The Republicans strongly criticized the deal. They said it was nothing more than taxes and a cut in defense. Most of all, the Republicans lamented the lack of presidential leadership. They felt double-crossed on taxes. The outrage seemed to be directed at Jim Baker. (Howard Baker had left early for a cabinet meeting.) The Republicans, knowing my own private views in all of this, were gentle on me. Privately, I empathized with them and in some respects felt like a traitor; my heart was with them.

As soon as the meeting could be concluded, Jim Baker and I sped down Pennsylvania Avenue to join the cabinet meeting, where the Bakers and I discussed the negotiations. Members of the cabinet were generally supportive, but they wanted to plot strategy in case the negotiations failed and there was a sequester.

The afternoon negotiating session on the Hill focused on the details of the numbers. Finally, at 4:30, the Democrats accepted my offer of an extra $0.1 billion cut in defense for 1988 in exchange for a $1.0 billion smaller cut for 1989.[28] The Speaker then came in and discussed the question of enforcement, saying that we must depend on "good faith." He said he was not sure it was a good idea to have a floor on defense spending for 1989: "Things may change; we could get a deal with the Soviet Union; technology may change." This was disheartening, for it suggested we didn't have a deal at all. But Jim Baker was able to get the tax writers to agree that the tax figure of $9.0 billion was gross, not net—that is, relative to the Gramm-Rudman-Hollings baseline—and would not be added to the taxes already approved in committee. We adjourned at 5:00, to reconvene that evening.

After a rare dinner in the White House mess, we returned to Capitol Hill for a session starting at 8:15. Following a brief discussion, Foley said that the technicians needed to discuss some matters in detail. We adjourned, subject to the call of the chair. The problem, of course, was that we were close to a deal but did not want people to go out and announce that a deal had been made before the principals had been given a chance to accept or reject it.

At the next morning's (November 20) White House operations meeting we discussed the negotiations. Howard Baker expressed optimism and said an agree-

---

[28] This would greatly ease the revisions in plans the Department of Defense would have to employ to meet lower spending levels.

ment was almost assured. I was less enthusiastic because I could not recommend that the president sign onto a deal unless it contained something more formal about enforcement.

At 9:15 we met with President Reagan. He expressed keen interest in what was going on, and we went over our plan. He asked about the revenue package. Jim Baker explained in broad terms what it would and would not contain. Howard Baker discussed the difficulty of getting a package passed by Congress, especially in light of the recalcitrance of the House Republicans. I made sure the president understood that we did *not* yet have an agreement over the enforcement mechanism and reported that I could not recommend that he accept the deal unless this defect were remedied.

The two Bakers and I met with Tom Foley in his office at 10:15 A.M. to discuss final issues. Foley said the Speaker wouldn't accept any written agreement—that that would be giving up cherished prerogatives of the House. However, according to Foley, he was otherwise willing to commit to anything we agreed on.

At 11:00, we met in Senate majority leader Byrd's office. The details of the revenue package were discussed and approved. On the spending side, I pointed out that a major problem was that the president had no assurance that the levels agreed to for defense and international affairs would actually be appropriated. I recommended that we write down the precise figures and agree to them. Wright responded that this would put defense and international affairs at a higher priority than programs for "poor folks, children, and so forth." I immediately offered to write down the numbers for all three categories, including domestic discretionary spending. Wright said he'd go along with that. Tom Foley then called a meeting of the negotiators for 12:30 P.M.

We have a deal!

After a quick lunch in Bob Dole's office, the negotiators met, with an hour to wrap up the enforcement mechanism. I took charge of the meeting and insisted on spelling out specific figures for domestic, international, and defense discretionary spending—both budget authority and budget outlays. Jamie Whitten again said he couldn't deliver. I responded that if we couldn't get assurance of that, there would be no deal. At that dramatic point, Foley agreed to my demand. I also insisted on OMB-approved scoring of the various measures Congress was to take to meet the terms of the agreement. I also pointed out that a sequester would take effect if congressional action fell significantly short of the terms of the agreement and that certain other provisions of the draft enforcement package were unacceptable. We then went on to other details.

A 2:30 meeting with the president was put off to 3:00. As we were about to leave to visit the president, a serious glitch arose when Danny Rostenkowski maintained that certain types of items previously agreed on would be unacceptable in the revenue package. Jim Baker was beside himself and took off for Rostenkowski's office (succeeding in bringing Rostenkowski around on the point but only after a phone chat between Rostenkowski and the president). I made final edits on the statement ultimately released and headed for the White House.

In the Oval Office I reported to the president that the package was acceptable, barely. The congressional leadership then came in, and the president reported that his advisers had just represented that the package met his requirements. There was polite general discussion, including kudos to Tom Foley. Then we went into the cabinet room to meet with the rest of the budget negotiators.

The president offered his congratulations. Speaker Wright noted that this was a bipartisan package, and Senate majority leader Byrd said it showed that the executive and the legislative branches could work together. Senate minority leader Bob Dole called it "a beginning," and House minority leader Bob Michel said it was a "good effort."

The president and the congressional leaders then went to the White House briefing room to say a few words and present the fact that we had an agreement to the world. Jim Baker and I then briefed the press on some of the package's details. Afterward, I returned press calls, granted a Public Broadcast Station television interview, and did Cable News Network's "Crossfire" show (which Bob Novak opened by demanding something to the effect, "Mr. Miller, aren't you ashamed of yourself for having sold out the American people?").

Later, I returned to the office, faced a mound of backed-up office work, ordered pizza, and left for home just before 10:00.

So, we had a package. Now we had to sell it.

8 | **Summit Aftermath**

OF ALL THE SENTIMENTS EXPRESSED during the budget summit, none was more prophetic than a remark by the group's chairman, Tom Foley. As we were pushing our chairs back from the table after agreeing on the package, Tom looked over at the three White House negotiators (Jim Baker, Howard Baker, and me) and said, "Now, you've got to help us get this thing passed!"

Of course, I knew all along that once we had a deal it would have to be passed by Congress. Indeed, throughout the negotiations, the congressional summiteers often used as an excuse for opposing a particular proposal not that they themselves couldn't accept it but that it would be impossible to sell to other members of Congress. Republicans couldn't sell tax increases; Democrats wanted tax increases but couldn't sell them unless they applied only to the rich. Republicans didn't want to cut Social Security; Democrats didn't either, but neither would they go along with cutting many domestic programs.

In one respect, however, I was shocked and dismayed by Foley's remark, for it reflected a tremendous imbalance in what the two sides brought to the bargaining table. Here we had been negotiating for twenty days and twenty nights (half the time Noah spent on the ark!). When *our* principal (President Reagan) said, "It's a deal," then it was a deal. But when the congressional leaders said, "It's a deal," it merely meant that they would encourage other members of Congress to vote for it. Although I didn't question the integrity of the congressional negotiators, I thought their constant harangues about President Reagan's "refusal to deal" altogether unfair, when they themselves were in no position to deal. In business, when you negotiate to sell something you don't have, it is known as fraud.

Selling the agreement

True to our commitment to help sell the package, the White House immediately revved up its sales campaign. This consisted of two elements: persuading individual members of Congress to support the package and persuading constituents to put pressure on members to support it. The agreement itself would reduce the deficit by $30.2 billion in fiscal year 1988—that is, compared with the Gramm-Rudman-Hollings (current services) baseline. Similarly, the budget agreement called for $45.8 billion in deficit reduction for 1989 (again relative to the Gramm-Rudman-Hollings baseline) for a grand, two-year total of "$76 billion in deficit reduction."

For 1988, $11.0 billion of the deficit reduction would be provided by increased revenues, including $9.0 billion in new taxes, $0.4 billion in user fees (such as increased fees for processing federal loans and use of the national parks), and $1.6 billion from increased Internal Revenue Service (IRS) enforcement (that is, increasing the IRS's budget so the agency could collect more taxes due).[1] On the outlay side, the defense budget would be reduced by $5.0 billion, domestic appropriated accounts would be reduced by $2.6 billion, and entitlement programs (Medicare, agriculture, guaranteed student loans, and so forth) would be reduced by $4.0 billion for a total of $11.6 billion. Other increased fees, asset sales, and a reduction in debt service (because of the lower deficit) would add another $7.6 billion to deficit reduction for 1988 (see figure 9). The amounts for 1989 were similar in composition: $17.3 billion for increased revenue, $20.0 billion for direct outlay reductions, and $8.6 billion for the rest for a total of $45.9 billion (again, see figure 9). Because a lot of oxen were getting gored in this package, and because the specific sources of the revenue and outlay changes had yet to be determined,[2] we had a large sales job to undertake.

---

[1] The topic of IRS enforcement should be of particular interest to economists and others, yet apparently little analytic work has been accomplished. More important than the question of net generation of funds to the federal government at the margin (for example, would an extra dollar given over to IRS enforcement generate $1, $2, $5, or $10 in taxes paid?) is the question of what resources *should* be devoted to IRS enforcement, recognizing that in a narrow sense the new taxes generated constitute a *transfer* of wealth whereas the efforts devoted to enforcement (plus the private efforts in response) constitute a use of real resources.

[2] For example, which taxes would be increased—taxes on business? taxes on personal income? taxes on "sin" (tobacco and alcohol)? How would the Medicare reductions be implemented—lower payments to doctors? to hospitals? a cutback in benefits?

Figure 9: Agreement Savings, 1988 and 1989

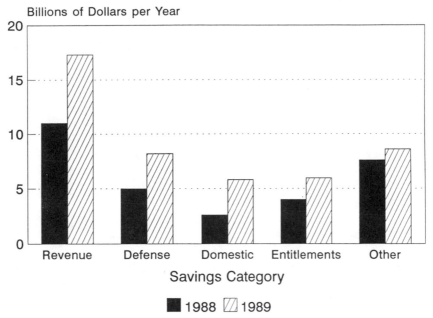

Billions of Dollars per Year

Savings Category

■ 1988 ▨ 1989

SOURCE: Office of Management and Budget

On November 21, the day after the agreement was announced, President Reagan devoted his Saturday radio address to explaining the budget summit compromise and urging people to support it. Working over the weekend, the White House staff began putting together materials in preparation for a blitz beginning on Monday. Thus, we prepared materials on how the agreement would affect state and local governments, the elderly, farmers, the business community, and so forth. The major line of argument was that although the agreement was not perfect, it was far better than the major alternative—a Gramm-Rudman-Hollings sequester. (Many of our materials told of the devastation that would occur should the Gramm-Rudman-Hollings robot be triggered into action.)

That same Saturday, Tom Foley and I appeared on CNN's "Newsmakers" interview show, where we both endorsed the agreement and encouraged members of Congress to support it. The next day, Foley appeared on CBS's "Face the Nation" (alongside Senator Phil Gramm), where he again supported the budget compromise. He also indicated publicly (as he had done privately) that it was necessary for Congress to meet the terms of the agreement fully to avoid a sequester. He also noted that whether Congress met this test would "be judged by the administration's own . . . Office of Management and Budget."

On Monday afternoon, the White House public liaison office assembled a group of high-powered business leaders in the cabinet room to hear from the president. After Howard Baker and I had briefed the ensemble, the president came in, assured them that the tax provisions in the package would be kept within bounds and that he would not accept tax increases that adversely affected the national economy. In response to a question from the president about how the agreement would be viewed by the stock market, John Phelan, the chairman of the New York Stock Exchange, responded that the market would approve because the agreement was preferable to a sequester and because the compromise reflected not the end, but the beginning, of a process of getting the federal deficit under control. Interestingly, the market showed little enthusiasm for the agreement, as the Dow-Jones was up a modest 9 points at the end of the day and the dollar edged downward.[3] But Monday also saw the first major "outside" endorsement of the plan—by the Republican Governors Association, chaired by New Jersey governor Thomas Kean.

Like other members of the administration, I was involved in a substantial public relations effort on behalf of the agreement. By Tuesday evening (November 24), I had appeared on PBS's "Nightly Business" show, CNN's "Crossfire," CNN's "Newsmakers," PBS's "MacNeil/Lehrer NewsHour," CNN's "Moneyline," BBC's "Money," C-Span's morning call-in show, and CBS radio. In addition, I'd given one-on-one interviews to reporters from *Time*, the *Wall Street Journal*, the *New York Times*, and the *Washington Post*.

Simultaneously, we sought to persuade individual members of Congress— especially Republicans—to support the agreement. Pursuant to a plan developed by the White House office of congressional affairs, the president placed telephone calls to Senators Byrd, Dole, and Simpson (R., Wyo.). Howard Baker talked with Senators Boschwitz (R., Minn.), Dominici, Gramm, Kassebaum (R., Kans.), and Rudman. Jim Baker called Senators Bentsen, Chaffee (R., R.I.), and Packwood. I called Senators Helms (R., N.C.), Nickles (R., Okla.), McClure, and Wallop (R., Wyo.). I also called Congressmen Lagomarsino (R., Calif.), Latta, Lewis (R., Calif.), and Martin (R., Ill.). Frank Carlucci called Senators Nunn (D., Ga.), Stennis (D., Miss.), Stevens (R., Alaska), and Warner (R., Va.). These were just the initial contacts, as numerous other phone calls and several meetings materialized during the week.

Understandably, many members of Congress opposed the budget compromise. Senator Kassebaum had sponsored a modified budget *freeze* (limiting, with few exceptions, appropriated accounts to zero increases), and she had substantial

---

[3] For an indication of the general reaction, see David R. Sands, "Market Barely Reacts to Budget Pact," *Washington Times*, November 24, 1987, and "Deficit Plan Reaction: Hohum," *Chicago Tribune*, November 24, 1987, p. A1.

support for this approach. Moreover, on Tuesday, November 24, Senator Armstrong sent out a "Dear Colleague" letter that blasted the budget agreement and called attention to its numerous shortcomings—particularly the fact that the budget deficit would not necessarily go down but would simply be lower than it might have been. The next day, Congressman Bill Gradison (R., Ohio) issued a "Dear Colleague" letter that expressed great consternation with the package and urged his colleagues to send the budget negotiators back to the bargaining table.

Because of certain provisions in the agreement (primarily tax increases opposed by Republicans and domestic cuts opposed by Democrats), a substantial revolt was brewing, and, as it turned out, enactment of the package was a fairly close thing. Indeed, the collective wisdom of the White House senior staff on Tuesday, November 24, was that roughly one-third of the members of the House of Representatives supported the package, one-third opposed it, and one-third were undecided. In the Senate the numbers were slightly more favorable, but because of the Senate rules allowing a filibuster, we needed to garner a great deal more support.

Enacting the package

President Reagan stayed active in the campaign to secure passage of the budget compromise.[4] He continued to meet with business and opinion leaders and directly lobbied members of Congress, sending a personal letter to each of them on November 27. Primarily as a result of the president's efforts, we received endorsements by the American Business Conference, the National Association of Manufacturers, the American Association of Retired Persons, the American Heart Association, the American Trucking Associations, the Business Round Table, and a plethora of small trade associations and individual companies, as well as an increasing number of members of Congress. We also obtained the endorsement of the bipartisan National Governors' Association, an effort organized by the group's chairman, Governor John H. Sununu of New Hampshire (later to become President Bush's chief of staff), and its vice-chairman, Governor Gerald L. Baliles of Virginia.

With momentum building for enactment of the budget compromise,[5] I

---

[4] See, for example, David Hoffman, "Reagan Ready to Lobby on Deficit Compromise," *Washington Post*, November 26, 1987, p. A4, and Gene Garbowski, "Reagan Lobbying for GOP Support of Deficit Package," *Washington Times*, December 1, 1987, p. A6.

[5] Although the momentum was clearly in our favor, substantial criticism of the accord continued. See, for example, Martin Feldstein, "Budget Card Tricks and Dollar Levitation," *Wall Street Journal*, December 1, 1987, p. 36, and Warren Brookes, "Playing Let's Pretend with the Deficit," *Washington Times*, December 1, 1987, p. F3.

turned my attention to two other matters: (a) making sure that Congress did, indeed, enact a package that generated the "savings"[6] we had all agreed on and (b) eliminating from the package what we in the administration considered objectionable provisions.[7] Controversy over the objectionable provisions came first. For example, consistent with a long-standing policy of the administration, I opposed a bailout of the railroad industry pension plan; although this proposal would not have technically increased the deficit for 1988, it would have cost taxpayers a bundle in the long run.[8] On December 15, I sent a letter to the congressional leadership, detailing what we considered particularly troublesome language in the appropriations measure then being fashioned to carry out the budget accord. The next day, I put together a list of the twelve most objectionable provisions—a list quickly dubbed the "dirty dozen."

For the most part, the provisions we objected to did not relate to spending programs but to restraints on the president's ability to run the government. (For example, on the list was a requirement that the Department of Defense buy U.S.-made computers, a requirement that equipment used for drilling on the outer continental shelf contain 50 percent U.S.-made materials, and a prohibition on the administration's implementing changes in family planning regulations that had just been issued by the Department of Health and Human Services.) It seemed as though many members of Congress took advantage of the budget agreement to shoehorn as many pet provisions into the omnibus appropriations bill as they could, thinking the president would be forced to approve the package because of his commitment to the budget compromise. However, the president made plain his resolve to veto the package if it were not cleared of extraneous provisions.[9]

The appropriations measure did, however, become "larded up" with excessive

---

[6] The provisions of the agreement were universally referred to as savings, even though half of them were designed to raise revenue; even the outlay provisions merely *slowed* the growth in spending rather than cut spending in an absolute sense (see discussion of baselines in chapter 10).

[7] During the negotiations, we had agreed to suspend our incessant criticizing of Congress for its excessive spending. But we pointedly had refrained from agreeing to terminate our criticisms of specific provisions. Thus, while we had no license to criticize the *size* of total spending (a figure that had been negotiated), we were perfectly at liberty to criticize and negotiate over specific items contained in the budget bills (both appropriations and reconciliation).

[8] See, for example, Paul Blustein, "Budget Chief Claims Tax Bill Aids Rail Lobby," *Washington Post*, December 10, 1987, p. D1.

[9] See, for example, Tom Kenworthy, "Reagan Threatens Veto of Deficit Pact," *Washington Post*, December 10, 1987, p. A8, and Jonathan Fuerberinger, "Reagan Veto of Deficit-Reducing Bill Is Threatened," *New York Times*, December 10, 1987, p. A25.

pork spending. Surprisingly, there seemed to be almost a direct relationship between the "tightness" of the appropriation (the need to reduce spending) and the lengths to which members of Congress would go to ensure the survival of their own pieces of pork. [10] On more than one occasion I had to inform a member of Congress who was prevailing on me to approve his particular project "in order to ensure his reelection" that to do so for this reason would constitute a violation of criminal law!

Of much greater concern to us was making sure that Congress did, indeed, enact a package that comported with the parameters of the budget summit compromise—that is, produced all the claimed deficit reduction. Although the sources of the savings were detailed in the agreement, several individual committees responsible for coming up with the savings began focusing on provisions that were patently phony, apparently in hopes I wouldn't see through them or that some other committee could be prevailed on to help them out. A favorite ploy was for a nonappropriations committee to reduce the amount authorized for a particular program and insist that I credit them with the savings. I would have nothing to do with such phony budgeting. [11]

One facet of the budget implementation we reviewed carefully was the savings on entitlement spending. These provisions, coming out of the Ways and Means/ Finance committees, proved to be a source of considerable controversy. Using their congressional staffs' much more optimistic projections, the committees came up with what they thought to be the required $4 billion in savings for each year, 1988 and 1989. I informed the committees that by our calculations their savings came close to the target for 1988 but fell far short for 1989. This drew a sharp rebuke from the committees. [12]

Another matter created even more controversy. According to the budget agreement, the Post Office and Civil Service committees of both Houses were to come up with savings of $850 million for both 1988 and 1989. From the discussions we had at the budget summit, I got the impression the committees would meet their obligation by restraining the growth of spending in the federal

---

[10] See, for example, Jeffrey H. Birnbaum and John E. Yang, "Congress Dulls Pain of Deficit-Cutting by Injecting Giveaways and Gimmicks," *Wall Street Journal*, December 14, 1987, p. 2.

[11] For example, suppose a specific program were in the spending baseline at $500 million and had been authorized for $600 million. The authorizing committee might propose reducing the authorization to $500 million and demand that $100 million in savings be credited to their action. This was phony, inasmuch as it would have had absolutely no effect on the level of spending and thus no effect on the level of deficit.

[12] See, for example, letter to me from Senate Finance Committee chairman Lloyd Bentsen (December 4, 1987).

personnel accounts (a freeze on hiring, limits on raises, and cuts in training expenses). Facing strong objections from the federal employee unions, however, the committees decided to take their savings out of the postal service accounts. Their initial proposals were phony—similar to the trick of reducing the authorization ceiling to something in excess of spending plans and calling this a savings. When I notified the committees that this was not a true savings, the congressional staffs asked what kinds of postal savings would be acceptable. My staff responded with a number of alternatives. The committees then chose a combination of alternatives that we accepted as generally meeting the requirements of the agreement.

At this point, however, the postal service responded with its version of the Washington Monument Game. On December 14, Postmaster General Preston R. Tisch announced that because of the pending action by Congress the postal service would suspend Saturday mail delivery, reduce window hours, and suspend weekend pickup and delivery. Facing hostile postal employees and disgruntled postal customers, the committees and postal service management suddenly began blaming it all on me personally, claiming that "OMB director Miller forced us to accept this in the deficit-reduction package."[13] Of course, I had not directed the committees' attention to the postal service, let alone mandated the particular cost-cutting measures the postal service announced.[14] Having set the problem up this way, the committees immediately proposed taking the postal service completely off budget. Because the postal service was running a deficit, this action would have reduced the on-budget deficit. Phony, phony, phony! In the end, my strong objections (threatening presidential veto) prevailed, and the committees forced the postal service to reduce its outlays.

All the time we were selling and orchestrating passage of the budget agreement, there were two other diversions. First, we faced a series of potential shutdowns because of an absence of appropriations. That is, many members of Congress, demanding action on the budget, agreed only to short-term extensions. On Wednesday, December 16, I sent a memorandum to agency heads telling them that we might well have to shut down by noon the next day. This threat was relieved by a two-day extension. Then on Friday, December 18, I sent the agencies a memorandum noting that appropriations would expire the next day and that initiatives would have to be taken to shut down all nonessential activities. Pursuant to an opinion rendered by the attorney general, however, shutdown

---

[13] The reason this argument gained currency is that I had been an outspoken critic of the postal service's monopoly over the delivery of addressed mail and its status as a government corporation.

[14] According to our calculations, the postal service could have realized the mandated savings merely by freezing employment in its headquarters operation in Washington. But why do that when other actions get far more attention?

procedures could commence on Monday, rather than on Saturday, so long as no additional federal funds were committed over the weekend. In response to a specific inquiry from the office of First Lady Nancy Reagan, we determined to keep the Washington Monument, the Smithsonian, and other Washington sight-seeing points open for business over the weekend. On Monday, December 20, Congress passed another extension of appropriations, averting yet another shutdown.

Second, we were in the midst of preparing a budget for 1989. In major respects, the preparation of this budget was made easy by having the parameters set forth before us in the two-year bipartisan agreement. For example, totals for defense spending and domestic discretionary spending were already established. However, what the president's priorities might be within those totals was the subject of great interest, and as word began to leak out about specific components of the draft budget, some controversy arose.

As an example, the draft budget incorporated a plan to establish the National Institutes of Health as a separate, nongovernment organization along the lines of the highly respected RAND Corporation—partly to enable it to pay higher salaries and therefore attract and retain the best talent. However, word of this leaked.[15] Asked about this at his daily briefing for the press on December 16, presidential spokesman Marlin Fitzwater noted that the plan had not been approved by me, much less the president, and characterized it as a "trial balloon."[16] Nevertheless, suspicions grew that the budget contained a lot of controversial provisions, which upset many members of Congress and made our efforts to get the agreement passed more difficult.

As we headed into the second half of December, and as members of Congress became antsy about their Christmas vacations, the budget package came together in a hurry. We at OMB were stretched to the limit, for in addition to our usual duties we were constantly updating our assessments of the budget packages Congress had under consideration. One thing we *didn't* want to happen was that Congress inadvertently send us a package that didn't meet the savings agreed on in the budget summit. Given one of the appropriations committee chairmen's oft-repeated protestations about the right of his committee to determine total spending (as opposed to having such determinations be made by budget sum-miteers, even though he was one), I was gravely concerned that the final figures—the totals for defense, international affairs, and domestic discretionary spending—would not be consistent with the budget agreement. As we came down to the wire, however, the appropriations committees did, generally, hit their targets for

---

[15] See, for example, Robert Pear, "Budget Plan Would Privatize National Institutes of Health," *New York Times*, December 16, 1987, p. A1.

[16] See, for example, "NIH May Go Private," United Press International, December 16, 1987.

Figure 10: Original versus Revised
Gramm-Rudman-Hollings Targets

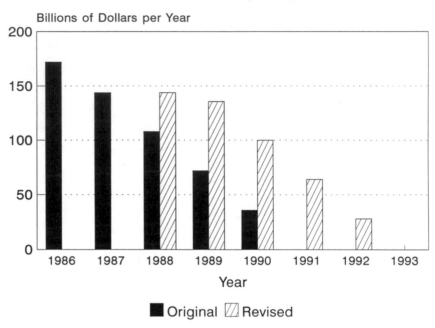

Billions of Dollars per Year

■ Original ▨ Revised

SOURCE: Office of Management and Budget

budget authority, although outlays proved to be higher than agreed to in the budget negotiations (see discussion later in this chapter). Moreover, while the Ways and Means/Finance committees did not enact sufficient legislative changes to realize the entitlement savings for 1989, they did come reasonably close to meeting their targets for 1988, at least by their forecasting methodology. Finally, in the wee hours of December 22—three months into the fiscal year—Congress passed a reconciliation bill and an appropriations measure to carry out the budget agreement and sent it to the president. The legislation also revised the Gramm-Rudman-Hollings deficit targets (see figure 10).

Later that day, I briefed the president in the Oval Office. I told him that, in general, the continuing resolution met the budget authority and projected budget outlay targets for defense, international affairs, and domestic discretionary spending by a narrow margin but that it contained numerous objectionable provisions, including excessive pork.[17] I told him that the reconciliation bill was much more

---

[17] See, for example, Gene Garbowski, "Catch-All Spending Bill Stuffed with Billions in Political Pork," *Washington Times*, December 30, 1987, p. A1.

troublesome—that although it contained all the tax increases we had agreed to, it fell short of meeting the agreement with respect to Medicare and asset sales; in addition, I noted that the bill contained expansions in the Medicaid program that would increase spending in future years. However, I told him that, given his commitment to a budget agreement and in view of the fact that we would have an opportunity to fix these shortcomings the following year, I would recommend that he sign the measure. He did so that afternoon, to the great relief of many members of Congress, some of whom had already left Washington for their Christmas vacations.

A tale of pork

With the enactment of appropriations consistent with the parameters of the budget agreement, a lot of people were disappointed. Biological scientists voiced concern that there was not enough in the budget to maintain America's leadership in this field. Space buffs took a setback. Almost everyone agreed the drug program needed more. Defense enthusiasts, who had seen a 50 percent buildup in this program, were shocked to realize that in the future the military would do well just to hold its own.

With many legitimate needs going unanswered, what began to stick in people's craw was the incredible amount of pork that had been stuffed in the budget just before enactment. The major focus of the ire was Senator Daniel K. Inouye, who had sponsored a provision to provide $8 million in subsidy to a little-known Jewish organization to construct a school in Paris to teach North African Jews.[18] (When Congress reconvened it promptly acted favorably on Senator Inouye's suggestion that this particular item be rescinded.)

Sensing an opportunity to drive home a point on which he had often spoken—the propensity of Congress to lard up appropriations with pork spending—President Reagan wanted to go on the offensive. However, he was constrained by the specifics of the budget agreement to spend the full amount allocated to domestic discretionary programs. We resolved that problem the following way: the president would request that Congress rescind spending on pork but put the money to better use—including the purposes for which an "emergency supplemental" was quickly being fashioned (increased spending for the war on drugs and so forth).

---

[18] Reportedly, a major contributor to Senator Inouye was a member of the organization's board of directors. See Joan Mower, "$8 Million to Build Jewish Schools in France," *Washington Post*, December 29, 1987, p. A13. In an editorial, the *Washington Post* characterized this initiative as the U.S. government's "most outrageous pay-out," January 3, 1988, p. B6.

So, in his State of the Union Message of January 25, 1988, President Reagan drew attention to the pork problem as follows:

> Over the past few weeks, we've all learned what was tucked away behind a little comma here and there. For example, there's millions for items such as cranberry research, blueberry research, the study of crawfish, and the commercialization of wildflowers. And that's not to mention the [half] million . . . so people from developing nations could come here to watch Congress at work.[19]

The president also noted that Congress had sent him a continuing resolution and a reconciliation bill with virtually no time to review either. Raising these massive documents into the air,[20] he declared, "Congress shouldn't send another one of these. No. And if you do, I will not sign it."[21] He then received a standing ovation from the very people who had sent the bills to him in the first place!

Working with an OMB draft (from which the president's examples had been gleaned), we compiled a list of pork that the president forwarded to Congress on March 10. This list was purposely conservative to avoid charges that the president was trying to undo the budget deal. However, the list identified dozens of pork initiatives that, if rescinded, would save (or put to better use) over a third of a billion dollars in 1988 and as much as $3.5 billion over the lifetimes of the projects. In addition, the package contained many items that most people would conclude were of low priority: $10 million for the Department of Agriculture to purchase surplus sunflower oil; $300,000 to provide a private underwater laboratory in Key Largo, Florida; $2.7 million to develop more efficient machinery for sewing men's tailored shirts; $19.2 million for the Department of Defense to increase its purchases of anthracite coal, when it already owned a four-year supply; $2.7 million for the Coast Guard to develop a portable sonar device, capable of detecting submarines, even though the agency has no wartime responsibilities; $500,000 for the Army Corp of Engineers to construct local recreation facilities in Des Moines, Iowa; and so forth.

This forty-six-page document landed on the desks of members of Congress with a dull thud and stayed there; after having sliced off the $8 million for Senator

---

[19] *Administration of Ronald Reagan*, 1988, p. 87.

[20] As many will recall, when President Reagan plopped one of those documents down on the nearby table he shook his hand, appearing to have mashed a finger. The next day, after a National Security Council meeting, I remarked, "Mr. President, you haven't lost a step when it comes to acting." "What do you mean?" the president asked. "I mean your dramatizing the weight of those bills last evening by imitating a mashed finger." "Oh, it's true," he said, "I cut my finger." And indeed he had, for he showed me the Band-Aid around the finger in question.

[21] *Administration of Ronald Reagan*, 1988, p. 87.

Inouye's project, Congress was not about to do any more paring. When it comes to pork, Congress's carving knife becomes dull quickly!

If Congress thought that was the end of the tale, it was mistaken. Five days later (March 15) I circulated a much longer pork list that created a massive controversy. Most pork is contained not in the individual appropriations bills but in the reports that accompany the bills when they are written in committee and brought to the floor for a vote. [22] Thus, it has become customary in Congress for such reports not only to explain the bills they accompany but also to direct the agencies to spend the money in particular ways. Although a bill may merely say that some agency has been appropriated X hundred million dollars for a general purpose, the committee report will direct the agency to spend so many million for this or that specific project. Because these reports are not presented to the president and are not subject to veto, the courts have held that the instructions they contain are not legally binding. In practice, however, agencies almost always go along with these congressional directives rather than risk the consequences. (Threats to cut the agency head's office staff are among the more common inducements.)

My memorandum to agency heads reminded them that congressional reports have no force of law (but also reminded them that appropriated funds must be spent to avoid violating the Impoundment Control Act). The memorandum, accompanied by a list of spending for their agencies mandated by committee reports, [23] also indicated that agency heads should not spend the money on those items without first clearing it with OMB. [24] Although eliminating these report-driven items would not have reduced the deficit, it would have allowed money to be spent for high-priority programs that did not receive the Midas touch of mention in an appropriations report.

Members of Congress, outraged by my attempt to deal with report-driven

---

[22] Identifying a piece of pork in an actual law gives the item too much visibility. Getting some sympathetic appropriations committee staff member to insert it in a routine report is much easier than getting a majority of the members of the committee to go on record in favor of it.

[23] The list included such gems as $400,000 for a project to find alternative commercial uses of oilseeds in North Dakota; $1.9 million to establish a mid-America world trade center in Wichita, Kansas; $2.0 million for the acquisition of land in Lake Tahoe, California, and Nevada; $1.7 million for the construction of a road to a private ski resort in Arizona; and $7.6 million for an underwater habitat in Saint Croix, Virgin Islands.

[24] One reason for the clearance requirement was to give the agency heads "cover." That is, coming under intense pressure from the appropriations committees and others in Congress to fund these pork programs, the agency heads could, in turn, blame OMB for not granting clearance.

spending, [25] retaliated by fashioning appropriations language designed to keep OMB from preventing or delaying the commitment of funds identified in committee reports. Because all spending is mentioned in such reports, this would have effectively nullified the limited spending control the president retained after the impoundment authority was eliminated during the dark days of Watergate. With Republicans leading the charge on Capitol Hill (the Democrats cleverly kept their heads down), and with no support from the West Wing ("Jim, this is your show"), I eventually capitulated, declaring that this was an issue the next president would have to resolve. [26]

Finalizing the 1989 budget

Given the White House's demonstrated inability to deal with pork in the budget and given that the major parameters of the budget had been established in the budget summit of October–November 1987, one would think that finalizing the 1989 budget would be straightforward. But Congress showed little inclination to bring the 1989 budget into line with the requirements of the budget summit. Indeed, as we shall see, just getting Congress to meet the Gramm-Rudman-Hollings deficit target and avoid a sequester was a damn close thing.

Despite pressure from the West Wing, I insisted that the president's budget submission for 1989 contain modifications in Medicare and other entitlement programs to meet the $4 billion in savings called for in the 1987 budget accord and to offset the cost of the expansions in entitlement programs that had been legislated since then. Chairman Bentsen of the Senate Finance Committee and Chairman Rostenkowski of House Ways and Means protested publicly and privately. In their defense, they were basing their claims on congressional staff figures showing that the savings that had been initiated the previous December carried over into the 1989 budget and fully met the requirements of the budget agreement. It was obvious to us at OMB, however, that the savings would not materialize because the congressional staff's estimates were altogether too optimistic.

Through the spring and summer we slogged along on the budget, testifying before congressional committees about individual proposals, answering questions about budget issues, and trying to effect spending priorities. Because of congres-

---

[25] The usually mild-mannered Senator Jim McClure responded, "I think he declared war on the Congress." See Joseph A. Davis, "War Declared over Report-Language Issue," *Congressional Quarterly*, June 25, 1988, p. 1752.

[26] See David Rapp, "OMB's Miller Backs Away from Report-Language Position," *Congressional Quarterly*, July 9, 1988, p. 1928, and "Miller Acts to End Feud with Hill over Funding," *Washington Post*, July 12, 1988, p. A21.

sional opposition to any spending cuts—even if they were arguably required by the budget agreement—by the end of the summer I had all but given up hope that the 1989 budget, as enacted, would fully reflect the agreement we had so laboriously negotiated in 1987 and to which we had religiously adhered. However, I was not about to allow myself to become an accomplice in Congress's violating the Gramm-Rudman-Hollings deficit target for that year—placed at $136 billion.[27]

In September 1988, I formally asked President Reagan to accept my resignation effective October 15, the day the final Gramm-Rudman-Hollings sequester report was due. Although it might seem that I chose to leave, and to leave on this particular date, to assure my independence of judgment, the major reason for my leaving government was financial.[28] We had three children in private schools, and even with Demaris's income it was not possible to live the life-style expected of a member of the president's cabinet.[29] Moreover, "I had done my thing"; it was time to leave and start a new life.

So, on September 26, the president announced to a large gathering in the Executive Office Building that he had accepted my letter of resignation and was appointing (per my recommendation) Joe Wright as my successor. He went to say some nice things about me and my contributions to his administration—to which I responded that it had been an extraordinary opportunity and honor to have served as his chairman of the FTC and director of OMB and that I appreciated his confidence. I also announced that I was looking forward to new opportunities with Citizens for a Sound Economy, George Mason University, and Capital Economics (a Washington, D.C., consulting firm).

Under Gramm-Rudman-Hollings II, the OMB director issues an initial sequester report on August 25 of each year. The report of August 1988, reflecting all the rules for compiling the Gramm-Rudman-Hollings baseline, concluded that the current-law deficit estimate (for 1989) was $144 billion—$8 billion over the $136 billion deficit target but $2 billion short of the sequester trigger of $146 billion.[30]

---

[27] With enactment of the 1988 budget, Congress revised the 1988 Gramm-Rudman-Hollings target from $108 billion to $144 billion and revised the 1989 target from $72 billion to $136 billion (see figure 10).

[28] I had told Vice-President Bush, Chief of Staff Howard Baker, and Deputy Chief of Staff Ken Duberstein of my plans to leave several months earlier. Baker and Duberstein had urged me to delay the announcement until after the GOP convention in August and then after the president returned from his West Coast vacation in September.

[29] The only other member of the cabinet living off current income was Secretary of Education Bill Bennett, and he and his wife had only one (preschool) child.

[30] The Gramm-Rudman-Hollings trigger has always been the deficit target plus a $10 billion margin of error.

Figure 11:   Target versus Actual Performance, 1988

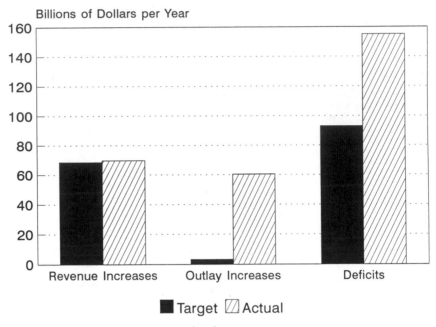

SOURCE: Office of Management and Budget

I knew, however, that the appropriations committees had developed bills that incorporated spending much in excess of the extrapolation of the previous year's spending that was incorporated in the Gramm-Rudman-Hollings baseline.[31] Unless the committees held this spending in check, there would be a sequester of at least $10 billion.[32] To communicate my firm resolve to call the figures as I saw them and to lessen the pressure from any source to overlook the obvious should spending rise to insupportable levels, I began a series of communications to the press, Congress, and the West Wing informing them of just where the projections were at any point in time. In particular, as time drew close to the publication of the final Gramm-Rudman-Hollings report (October 15), I sent the

---

[31] Until appropriations for a year have been enacted, the spending level incorporated in the Gramm-Rudman-Hollings baseline is the previous year's spending level adjusted for inflation.

[32] If the deficit estimate exceeds the trigger, the Gramm-Rudman-Hollings robot cuts spending enough to bring the deficit down to the target.

Figure 12: Target versus Actual Performance, 1989

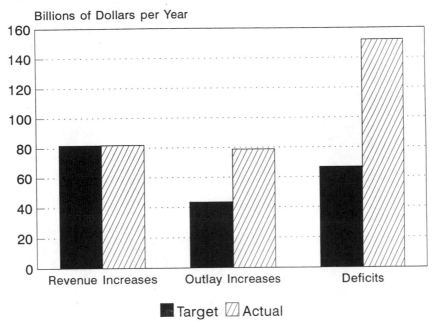

SOURCE: Office of Management and Budget

chairmen and ranking members of the Ways and Means/Finance and appropriations committees, as well as the congressional leadership, a letter almost every day explaining how their latest decisions had affected the deficit estimate.

Given previous congressional behavior and knowing something about the incentives faced by individual members of Congress, I expected that, on final enactment of the 1989 budget, the deficit estimate would be reasonably close to the Gramm-Rudman-Hollings trigger. That is, given a limit, Congress will spend all the money. Indeed that was so, for our analysis of October 15 showed a revised deficit estimate of $145.5 billion—half a billion dollars less than the $146 billion sequester trigger and $9.5 billion over the deficit target.

On October 15 (a Saturday), I walked over to the Oval Office, gave the president the Gramm-Rudman-Hollings final sequester report, affirmed to him that no sequester would be necessary, listened to him record his weekly radio address, and bid him adieu. Then Demaris and I had lunch for a final time in the White House mess and, as we went out the front gate, left behind nearly eight years of government service.

Figure 13:   Federal Deficits, 1986–1989

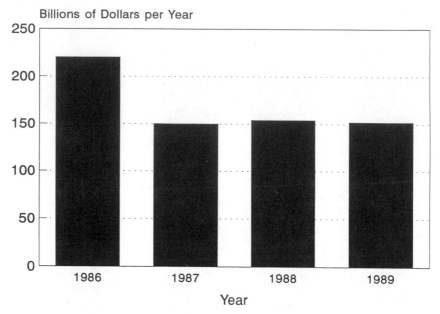

SOURCE: Office of Management and Budget

Retrospective

The 1987 budget summit concluded in a two-year agreement, for 1988 and 1989. According to the terms of the compromise, the administration agreed to a tax increase in exchange for certain budget cuts relative to the Gramm-Rudman-Hollings (current services) baseline. The claim of the summiteers was that over two years there would be "$76 billion in real deficit reduction."

Yet, what really happened? Under the agreement, compared with OMB's midsession review baseline, receipts were supposed to increase by $68.6 billion for 1988 and $81.8 billion for 1989.[33] The actual increases were $69.8 billion in 1988 and $81.8 billion in 1989 (see figures 11 and 12). So, the congressional leadership pretty much got its increased revenue. But what about the restraints on spending? Under the agreement, outlays were supposed to go up by $3.3

---

[33] I use the OMB current services baseline for this two-year comparison because at the time of the agreement there did not exist a Gramm-Rudman-Hollings baseline for 1989.

billion in 1988 and $43.6 billion in 1989. Instead, they went up a whopping $60.3 billion in 1988 and $78.8 billion in 1989.

The bottom line is that in 1987, when President Reagan held firm against invitations to deal and threatened to veto any tax increase or appropriations he deemed excessive, the deficit fell a record $71.5 billion (from $221.2 billion to $149.7 billion). But when he was persuaded to go along with congressional demands for a budget summit, the public got additional taxes, an unleashing of spending growth, and no further progress on the deficit (see figure 13).

Why did the president go along with this budget deal? After all, he had been taken by budget deals in the past. (He often railed, in reference to the 1982 budget deal, "I was promised $3 in spending cuts for every $1 in tax increases; I got the taxes but none of the spending cuts!") Quite simply, he was in a weakened position vis-à-vis Congress and unable to resist the demands of its leadership.

The reason for this state of affairs is that, in November 1986, the president and Ed Meese announced the summary details of a scandal that became known as "Irangate"—the exchange of hostages for arms and the diversion of payments to help fund the *contras* in Nicaragua. This harebrained scheme cost the president and his administration dearly. The uncertainty about direct presidential involvement (and, if so, the likelihood of impeachment) hung over the White House like a cloud. The efforts of some of the administration's best and brightest were diverted into coping with each day's new revelations and searching for the truth. New initiatives were either postponed or fell on deaf ears. Ongoing programs (for example, privatization) became increasingly boxed in by congressional directives we couldn't overcome.

In short, during the last two years of the Reagan administration we were entirely on the defensive. Irangate created many casualties—one of which was further progress on the deficit.

9 | **The Bush and Clinton Budgets**

Dᴇꜱᴘɪᴛᴇ ᴛʜᴇ ᴅɪꜱᴀᴘᴘᴏɪɴᴛɪɴɢ ʟᴀᴄᴋ ᴏꜰ ᴘʀᴏɢʀᴇꜱꜱ on the deficit at the very end of the Reagan administration, there was reason for optimism when George Bush was sworn into office. The reason, as explained in chapter 8, is that Congress had agreed to revised Gramm-Rudman-Hollings targets—which were less than $100 billion for 1990—leading to a balanced budget by 1993.

Perhaps more important, in light of the substantial deescalation of tensions between the superpowers, George Bush took a very different approach to military spending than did Ronald Reagan. Under Gramm-Rudman-Hollings, defense spending was Reagan's Achilles' heel. When President Reagan would threaten to veto revenue measures, the big domestic spenders on Capitol Hill would say, "OK, Mr. President, I guess we'll just have to have a sequester—and, as you know, 50 percent will come out of defense." This was a powerful ploy, and although the president never fully caved in, he was usually softened by this tactic.

In contrast, President Bush was of a mind to accept some reduction in defense appropriations. Accordingly, the threat used on Reagan simply wouldn't work on Bush. Indeed, under the Gramm-Rudman-Hollings rules, Bush would likely get more for defense if there were a sequester than if he went along with the conventional budget process.

The Bush budgets

Soon after taking office, President Bush addressed Congress and asked for revisions in the Reagan budget proposal for 1990 to make it "kinder and gentler." For the most part, this amounted to rearranging priorities. Vis-à-vis Reagan, Bush trimmed defense and increased spending on education and the environment. Interestingly, because Bush proposed spending more than was spent in 1989 but less than current services for 1990, he was criticized by some for cutting spending and by others for increasing spending depending on which baseline was used.

Bush's first major budget, for 1991, was fairly conventional in approach. Its notable feature was that it contemplated significant deficit reduction: from the 1989 figure of $152 billion, down to $93 billion—just below the Gramm-Rudman-Hollings target for the year. In a message accompanying the budget, OMB director Dick Darman emphasized the limits of federal resources and urged everyone, including the media, to focus on actual spending levels, not cuts from current services.

At this point, the president and his associates could adopt one of two basic strategies. They could contest the budget by establishing certain parameters (including "read my lips: no new taxes") and then rely on the threat of a sequester to coerce Congress into meeting lower deficits targets by means of restraints on spending. The other approach was to *cut a budget deal*. They chose to cut a deal.

Why? First, Congress wanted to negotiate. Everything else being equal, the congressional leadership prefers a negotiated budget because (from their standpoint) they tend to get a better outcome in terms of policy and get in more on the action. Second, Director Darman was convinced he could negotiate a multiyear deal that would allow Bush to solve the deficit problem once and for all.

During the spring and early summer Darman and the president's chief of staff, John Sununu, discussed the 1991 budget with the congressional leadership, but negotiations made little progress. In June, the congressional leadership met with the president and reported that there would be no settlement unless he demonstrated some flexibility on the issue of taxes. It was at this point that Bush indicated that taxes would be on the table but that he wasn't interested in a settlement involving any new taxes. Budget negotiations then commenced in earnest.

During the first week of July, Saddam Hussein and his henchmen invaded Kuwait, triggering a series of events that culminated in the gulf war. A national debate emerged, with many urging the administration to be aggressive and others urging caution. It was plain, however, that the president would not let the incursion stand and that, to accomplish his goals, he would eventually have to have the acquiescence of Congress.

Budget negotiations dragged on during the summer but quickened after Congress's August recess, with the end of the fiscal year looming. After marathon sessions at nearby Andrews Air Force Base, it became clear that the *best* deal the president's men could get involved significant new taxes. At this point, President Bush was in a box. He could reject the budget deal and go to the people on the issue of new taxes in the November elections. Or he could accept the budget deal and, in the process, violate his famous pledge.

What tilted the decision was that the administration was now knee-deep in sand in the gulf, and the president needed a bipartisan Congress to achieve his

Figure 14: Federal Revenues, 1990 to 1993

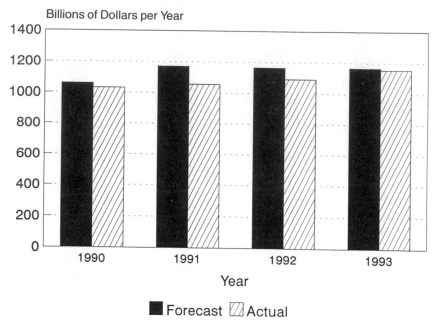

Billions of Dollars per Year

■ Forecast ⊠ Actual

SOURCE: Office of Management and Budget

goals in the region. If he rejected the budget deal and made taxes a partisan issue in the election, he risked losing the foreign policy support he desperately needed. Bush opted for the budget deal, arguing that "changed circumstances" necessitated his breaking his pledge on taxes.

The budget deal of September, however, faced significant opposition, and an unusual coalition of liberals opposed to spending cuts and conservatives opposed to tax increases combined to defeat the measure when it came before the House of Representatives. After some modifications that softened the spending cuts and raised taxes on those with higher incomes, the bill passed, and the president signed it into law.

What was the result of this "deal of the century," which was meant to reduce the deficit by $500 billion over five years? Federal revenues fell significantly below forecast (see figure 14) for two reasons. First, the official forecasters—the Office of Management and Budget, the Congressional Budget Office, and the Congressional Joint Committee on Taxation—use variants of what may be termed *static modeling*. That is, their forecasting models do not take sufficient account of the fact that, faced with alterations in tax incentives, people will change their behav-

Figure 15:   Federal Outlays, 1990 to 1993

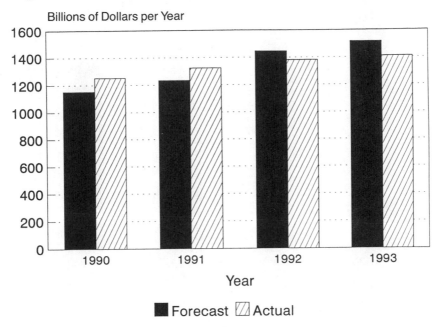

Forecast **Actual**

Source: Office of Management and Budget

ior. They will earn less or shelter their income from taxes, for example. So, even at higher tax rates, federal revenues fell below forecast.

The second, more important reason for the shortfall in revenue is that just as the negotiators at Andrews Air Force Base were working their magic, the U.S. economy entered a recession. Because federal revenues are closely linked with economic growth, the deficiency in nominal output led to a significant shortfall in revenues.

In contrast, during 1990 and 1991 federal outlays ran ahead of forecast, though this trend was reversed in 1992 and 1993 (see figure 15). Part of the reason for the higher spending is that, with higher unemployment in 1990 and 1991, federal outlays for certain "safety net" entitlement programs were higher than scheduled. Another reason is the inherent bias that official forecasters seem to have with respect to outlays—especially when the budget is the result of a deal and the deal makers are scrounging for the last dime, so they can claim to have met some deficit-reduction target. Also, no matter what safeguards are built into the budget process, Congress can usually find a way around them and increase spending for valued constituents.

Figure 16:   Federal Deficits, 1990 to 1993

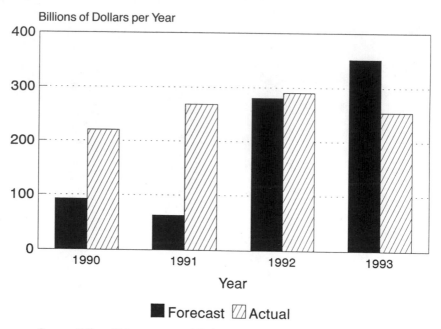

SOURCE: Office of Management and Budget

Outlays were less than forecast in 1992 and 1993, but the major reason was that the Resolution Trust Corporation lagged behind schedule in bailing out (and closing down) bankrupt thrift institutions. This put some outlays over into the next year(s). Also, inflation was lower than forecast.

With revenues falling short and outlays running ahead, the deficit substantially outpaced forecast, at least initially. Moreover, rather than falling, as promised under the budget deal, deficits actually rose through 1992 (see figure 16).

The 1990 budget deal did, however, incorporate some innovative spending caps and other controls that would have pressed the deficit downward. Unfortunately, these were to become effective for the 1993 budget, and almost immediately on taking office President Clinton voided these restraints, preferring his own approach to deficit reduction.

Clinton's budget deal

During the campaign of 1992, Governor Clinton made the deficit a major issue and promised to make it as well as the economy a top priority. On February 17,

1993, the administration released A *Vision of Change for America*, which contained the outlines of its budget for 1994 and beyond, including changes in the previously enacted 1993 budget. Then, on April 8, the administration released the formal budget.

President Clinton's vision included an economic stimulus program (primarily increased spending during 1993 on public works and job training), a significant increase in tax rates on those in higher-income brackets, and a further reduction in defense spending, the proceeds of which would be used to fund increases in domestic spending. The vision did not include any details on the president's proposed reform of health care financing.

After much public debate, the president's economic stimulus program went down to defeat when Democrats were unable to force cloture on a Republican effort to filibuster the measure. Tactically, the president had made a major mistake by refusing even to talk with Republicans about his proposal, much less involve them in negotiations. This slight held the Republicans together and forced the president's retreat.

The president's overall deal fared much better, though it was a close call. The votes on the separate versions of the reconciliation bill during July were close: a six-vote margin in the House and one vote in the Senate, with Vice-President Gore breaking a tie. In August, the votes on the conference report (agreement between the Houses) was even closer, with a two-vote margin in the House and another tie-breaking vote in the Senate.

What are we to make of yet another $500 billion deficit-reduction deal? Simply, it's not as advertised and in all likelihood will fall far short of meeting the stated objective. First, despite all the rhetoric about spending cuts, nominal spending rises every year (see figure 17). So do federal revenues. In fact, federal revenues would rise even without the increases expected from the changes in the tax code. Also, although the deficit is expected to decline somewhat, it rises again at the end of the period. Moreover, never does the deficit fall to the levels of 1987–1989.

On the whole, the forecast for the budget deal is indefensibly optimistic. The tax rate increases are likely to dampen economic activity, and thus the additional federal revenue from economic growth will be less than predicted. The base to which the new taxes apply will be lower also, so the increment from the changes in the tax code will turn out to be less than forecast.

The pattern of reductions in outlays from current services gives one little cause for optimism, for the major savings don't materialize until the last two years of the deal—1997 and 1998. In fact, there are virtually no savings during the first three years of the deal (counting changes for 1993). If the economy is less robust than forecast, then outlays for entitlements will be higher than scheduled. Finally, it is unlikely that Congress will find it possible to live within the

Figure 17:   Budget Deal, 1993

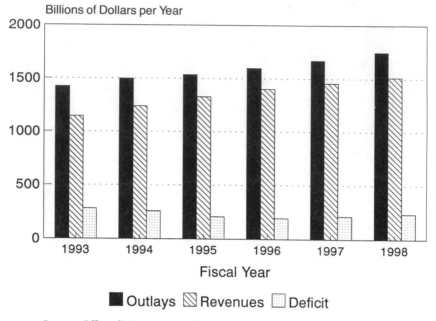

Billions of Dollars per Year

Fiscal Year

■ Outlays ⧅ Revenues ▢ Deficit

SOURCE: Office of Management and Budget

spending limits incorporated in the deal. Spending will rise—especially if an ambitious health care financing program is put on the table—and deficit progress almost certainly will be nil.

In short, two $500 billion deficit-reduction deals in a row have not, and will not, solve the deficit problem. Is there any hope?

10 | Why the U.S. Budget Has Failed

THE PREVIOUS CHAPTERS of this book should be enough to persuade even the most optimistic Washington insider that the U.S. budget system has failed. In particular, the existing institutional arrangement has failed to curtail deficit finance. Because federal spending has outrun federal revenue in all but one of the past twenty-five years,[1] it should be apparent that deficits are not an aberration; they are indigenous to the current budget system.

The budget system has also failed to rein in federal taxes. Despite a decade during which tax cuts and tax simplification dominated the revenue side of the fiscal agenda, federal tax revenue has grown inexorably and is now at the highest level in history. In 1990, the per capita tax burden was $4,300.[2] In 1980, it was $2,300. That's an 87 percent increase.[3]

Moreover, the budget system has failed to stem the march of excessive spending. Despite a decade during which the White House has been occupied by two of the most conservative presidents in this century, and despite an electorate sensitized about excessive spending by virtue of the Grace Commission Report[4] (stories of $500 toilet seats and the like), per capita federal spending is greater than ever before. In 1990 it exceeded $4,800 for every man, woman, and child. In 1980, per capita spending was $2,600. That's an 85 percent increase.[5]

---

[1] The exception was a small $3.2 billion surplus in 1969.

[2] Source of data on population: Bureau of the Census, U.S. Department of Commerce, *Statistical Abstract of the U.S. 1990.*

[3] In real terms, the increase was 44 percent.

[4] See *President's Private Sector Survey on Cost Control: A Report to the President* (January 17, 1984).

[5] In real terms, the increase was 43 percent.

At least as troubling to some is the failure of our budget system to provide an acceptable *structure* of taxes and spending. The proportion of federal revenue generated by payroll taxes has increased from 31 percent to 36 percent in only ten years, giving rise to charges that the system has become highly regressive.[6] Moreover, the incidence of taxes is poorly understood. Although most people are generally aware of the income and Social Security taxes they pay, they believe that taxes on corporations are paid by someone else. In fact, as President Reagan frequently pointed out, corporations don't pay taxes, people pay taxes.

The budget system has also failed to mesh the public's demands with available resources—that is, to establish acceptable budget priorities. The heavy contributors to politicians get their initiatives greased. Special interests lobby successfully to protect their own pieces of the pie. Worthless, and even counterproductive, programs live on and on, and desperate needs go wanting.

To most members of Congress, the budget system has failed because enacting the year's budget consumes an ever-increasing portion of their time in what is clearly wasted effort. The *appropriators* (members of the appropriations committees) blame the *budgeteers* (members of the budget committees) for not preparing the budget resolution on time. The budgeteers complain that the appropriators and the *reconcilers* (members of the Ways and Means and Finance committees) do not follow their instructions. And the reconcilers charge that the budgeteers and the appropriators throw off on them the hard work of cutting entitlement programs and raising taxes. Members of Congress who are not directly involved in the budget process consider those who are out to lunch.

If members of Congress find the budget process maddening and confusing, that goes double for the American public. The budget is somewhat technical, to be sure—in fact, far more technical than it needs to be. But the amount of budget ignorance abroad in the land is surprising, given the importance of budget decision making on people's daily lives. Some of that ignorance is understandable, however, given the propensity of politicians to mislead and obfuscate the budget for their own purposes.

The previous chapters illustrate some major failings of the current budget system. But there are problems that were not addressed. Why, for example, do we suddenly discover that we have a savings and loan crisis? Covering the federal guarantee on savings and loan deposits will end up costing American taxpayers much more than a king's ransom, with estimates ranging from $136 billion to $500 billion, after interest payments are included—or from $544 to $2,000 for

---

[6] A tax system is said to be regressive when those of higher income pay a lower *proportion* of their income in taxes.

each person in the country.[7] What is more, there are even greater liabilities in the federal budget, and few politicians have the courage to address them.

This chapter describes the three major reasons for the budget's failure. The first is a lack of truth in budgeting. At best our leaders fail to disclose fully what's in the budget, and at worst they misrepresent it. The second major reason for the budget's failure is the widespread acceptance of certain myths about the budget. The third, and even more important, major reason for failure is the institutional framework of the U.S. budget—specifically, deficiencies that explain to a large extent the chronic tendency toward deficit finance, burgeoning taxes, and excessive spending.[8]

Throughout the discussion that follows, it will help to think of the federal budget as analogous to your own personal budget or, better yet, to think of someone doing your budgeting for you. Wouldn't you want to know the sources of revenue and what was being spent? And wouldn't you want to set some guidelines about revenues, spending, and priorities? You should demand no less when it comes to the federal budget.

Absence of truth in budgeting

Of all the problems faced by the public in comprehending the U.S. budget and evaluating how their elected representatives deal with it, none is more vexing than the widespread confusion between actual spending and what is known technically as *current services*.

When Larry Lunchpail and Louise Lawyer sit down and go over the family financial crisis, their approach is different from that of the Washington insiders[9] when they address the federal deficit. Larry and Louise say, "We've got to cut spending." They will decide to eat out twice a month rather than once a week, purchase a new refrigerator *or* a new TV but not both, and postpone buying a new car. They may also say, "We've got to make more money." Larry will volunteer to take on more overtime at his construction job; Louise will offer to hustle a bit

---

[7] Estimates of the cost of the savings and loan bailout range widely. See, for example, Paul Duke, Jr., "Little Restitution from S&L Fraud Expected by U.S.," *Wall Street Journal*, July 25, 1990, p. A2.

[8] For a different, though generally consistent, perspective on the failure of the budget process, see John F. Cogan, *Federal Budget Deficits: What's Wrong with the Congressional Budget Process*, Essays in Public Policy series (Stanford: Hoover Institution Press, 1992).

[9] The term is meant to include not only elected representatives but unelected officials and, especially, the Washington-based media.

more and bill a few more client hours. But the framework for their discussion will be next month's budget versus this month's or next years's budget versus this year's.

Not so for the Washington insiders. When they talk about cutting spending next year, they don't mean spending less than this year. They mean spending less than *would* be the case if spending were left on automatic pilot—a level known technically as current services spending. In forming the starting point for spending, the Washington insiders first take last year's spending on entitlement programs and adjust that figure for inflation. Then, they inflate entitlements again to reflect demographic factors (such as more people eligible for Social Security and Medicare) and other variables (such as more students wanting government-subsidized loans). Then they add this onto every new entitlement program (and expansions in existing programs) they've legislated in previous years. Of course, when it comes to appropriated accounts (the other half of spending), they bend the rules and *assume* that these programs will be funded and then adjust last year's levels for inflation.

To give you an idea of how this works, in the Bush budget for 1991, released on January 29, 1990, OMB forecasted that total spending for fiscal year 1990 would be $1.197 trillion[10] (see figure 18). The inflated current services spending level for 1991 was $1.241 trillion—a difference of $44 billion. Now suppose Congress had enacted President Bush's budget for 1991, which called for spending to be $1.233 trillion. The Washington insiders would say this was a *cut* of $8 billion. But Larry and Louise would know that it was actually an *increase* of $36 billion.

Washington insiders do the same thing for tax revenues. When they talk about a revenue increase, they are not talking about increasing the level of taxes paid over the amount generated this year; they are talking about increasing taxes over and above an inflated, current services estimate for next year. To give you an idea of what is at stake, in that same Bush budget OMB estimated that 1990 federal tax revenues would be $1.074 trillion. But to this figure the Washington insiders added the expected additional taxes that would be paid in 1991 because more people would be at work and paying taxes, people already at work would be earning more and paying higher income taxes, businesses would be paying higher payroll taxes as well as higher income taxes, and everybody would be paying higher excise taxes. OMB estimated this total amount for 1991 to be $1.156 trillion—$82 billion more than in 1989. In other words, left on automatic pilot, the tax code would extract $82 billion more in taxes than it did in 1990. Some in Washington call this the starting point. But $82 billion is more, in *real*

---

[10] Source of budget data in this and the following paragraph: *Budget of the United States Government, Fiscal Year 1991*, pp. A-27 and A-283.

Figure 18:   Actual versus Current Services

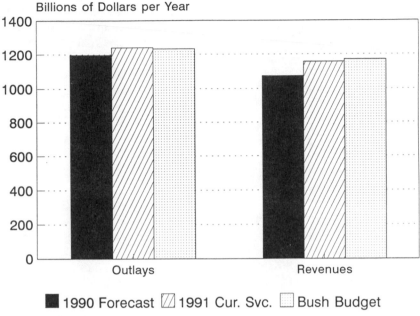

Billions of Dollars per Year

■ 1990 Forecast ▨ 1991 Cur. Svc. ▢ Bush Budget

Source: Office of Management and Budget

terms, than the entire U.S. government spent in 1951! And even though President Bush proposed to have the 1991 revenue increase total $96 billion (in other words, the $82 billion automatic increase plus an extra $14 billion), the congressional leadership demanded new revenues and forced the president go back on his pledge not to raise taxes.

Only in Washington can people engage in Orwellian Newspeak and get away with it. A spending increase is really a cut. And $82 billion more in tax revenue is not really an increase at all. Constant harping on budget cuts that are actually increases lowers the public's opposition to new spending. Frequent calls for new revenue to finance pressing needs or to reduce the deficit when, in fact, there is usually ample new revenue to accommodate both objectives eases the public's resistance to tax increases.

The second truth in budgeting deficiency is the scant attention given to the enormous liabilities hanging over every taxpayer. Although mention of these is included in the budget, they are almost never discussed until something happens and those responsible engage in an orgy of finger pointing and mutual recriminations. Although it may be difficult to estimate these liabilities precisely, they are *huge*.

There are two kinds of liabilities: those that we know we will have to pay eventually and that we *may* have to pay. Among the liabilities that we know we will have to pay is the national debt. Reflecting to a major extent a standoff between presidents opposed to tax increases and a congressional leadership determined to increase spending, the debt tripled over the decade of the 1980s— from $709 billion in 1980 to $2,299 billion in 1990.[11] This debt, high by historical standards, represents a substantial burden on future generations. Whether we pay it off (as we probably should) or simply let the matter ride should be a product of intelligent discourse rather than the sloganeering that presently obfuscates the true issue.

Although interest on the debt shows up clearly in budget accounts, the costs of some important unfunded liabilities do not, the most important of which is Social Security. The Ponzi scheme[12] known as Social Security is one of the most explosive issues and misunderstood institutions in contemporary America. The stakes in this system are enormous. Social Security constitutes more than one-fifth of the federal budget, but no politician dares fiddle with the program for fear of being turned out of office. Like all Ponzi schemes, Social Security works well when there is a broad base of payers and a narrow apex of beneficiaries. But demographics are reversing this situation; tomorrow's payees will bear tremendous Social Security taxes to support their tomorrow's beneficiaries. This situation could well bring on decades of intergenerational strife in the first third of the next century.

Moreover, the Social Security trust fund continues to finance current spending rather than set aside money for the future. *By law*, the Social Security trustees may invest only in government bonds, which *automatically* finances current spending because the proceeds from those bonds go into the Treasury as revenue. Unless something is done, when the Social Security trust fund is needed to pay benefits to baby boomers during the second and third decades of the next century, the trust fund's only asset will be IOU's on those current taxpayers.[13]

Medicare, which covers approximately 30 million aged and 3.3 million disabled Americans, is a large, unfunded liability under present circumstances. Like Social Security, Medicare's hospital insurance fund is presently running a

---

[11] Ibid., p. A-304. This is the so-called external debt—the debt held by the public; it does not include debt held in federal government accounts. In constant (inflation-adjusted) dollars, the deficit approximately doubled over the decade.

[12] A Ponzi scheme is the same as a chain letter: Those currently receiving benefits are receiving them from those currently paying into the system. Those currently paying will receive benefits only if new participants are found and incorporated.

[13] The budget deal of 1990 (that is, the Omnibus Budget Reconciliation Act of 1990) did not change this aspect of Social Security financing.

surplus, but its current revenues will quickly be eclipsed by increased outlays. According to OMB, the system could require a doubling of revenues by the year 2050.[14]

Although not as large as the hospital insurance program (at an estimated $60 billion in 1991), Medicare's $47 billion supplementary medical insurance program is likewise in trouble in the following sense: although it is funded each year and technically would be terminated if it didn't receive appropriations, this program will continue well into the future. Medicare premiums currently cover only one-quarter of the cost of this program, so as it escalates in response to an aging population, the demands on the budget will be severe.

Fortunately, the civilian and military pension systems are reasonably self-financing—that is, contributions by current employees offset benefits paid to retirees. Assuming that government employment does not diminish over the coming decades, this program is in fairly good shape. However, the prospect of substantial cutbacks in military personnel could mean a substantial portion of this program ($22 billion in 1991) will need support from the federal Treasury.

These are the commitments that must be paid. Far more troublesome to many are the commitments by the federal government to *underwrite* credit and insurance programs entailing much larger sums that *may* have to be paid. Everyone knows, of course, about the savings and loan insurance commitment. But at $959 billion in 1989, this commitment is only about half the $1.8 trillion federal commitment to cover bank deposits. In addition there is $162 billion of credit union deposit insurance (see figure 19).

The government has several other insurance programs for which there are outstanding liabilities. The 1989 face values of these liabilities were $820 billion for private pension insurance, $228 billion for aviation war risk insurance (which would pay off owners of aircraft in case of destruction due to acts of war), $179 billion for flood insurance, and $60 billion for veterans' life insurance, federal crop insurance, maritime war risk insurance, and overseas private investment insurance (which would pay off for certain assets seized in time of war) (see figure 20). The total face value of major federal insurance programs is $4.2 trillion.[15] That liability is almost double the national debt!

In addition, the federal government has a massive credit program—direct loans, loan guarantees, and loans to so-called government-sponsored enterprises (GSEs). The largest *potential* liability relates to the $763 billion loaned to GSEs (see figure 21). Although it is unlikely that the major ones, including the Government National Mortgage Association (Ginnie Mae), the Federal National Mortgage Association (Fannie Mae), and the Federal Home Loan Mortgage

---

[14] *Budget of the United States Government, Fiscal Year 1991*, p. 226.

[15] Ibid., p. 247.

Figure 19:   Federal Deposit Insurance, 1989

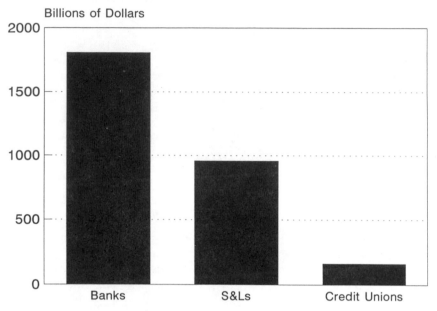

Billions of Dollars

SOURCE: Office of Management and Budget

Corporation (Freddie Mac), would fail (if they did they would require a substantial payoff from the federal Treasury, given their large asset base), the scope of the liability is obvious.

Second in size among the government's credit programs is its outstanding loan guarantees, amounting to $588 billion. The Chrysler bailout of the mid-1970s is an example of a successful loan guarantee—one that was not invoked because the borrower paid off. But many loan guarantees are invoked, and *potentially* the taxpayer could be required to pay off more than half a trillion dollars in the (unlikely) event all defaulted.[16]

Then, of course, there is the government's direct loan program, of which $207 billion was outstanding in 1989. These are direct loans made to private individuals, companies (primarily small businesses), and certain government entities. Although under these programs the government constitutes "the lender

---

[16] Included in each year's federal budget are sums to defray the costs of defaulted loans. But estimating that figure is a difficult task, and actual sums often differ starkly with the sums included in the budget.

Figure 20:   Other Federal Insurance, 1989

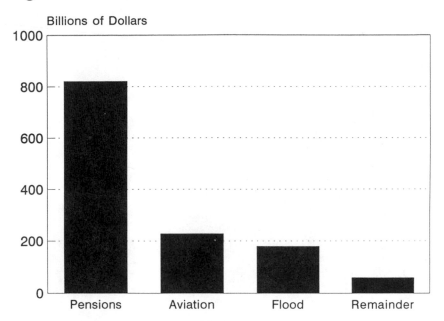

SOURCE: Office of Management and Budget

of last resort," they are defended by their congressional proponents as not costing anything. The truth lies somewhere in between. Many of the recipients of these loans *could* obtain loans from commercial sources; they don't because government loans can be obtained at much more favorable rates. Moreover, the default rate on government loans is much higher than any private financial institution could tolerate. On average, OMB estimates that the annual subsidy in the direct loan program is on the order of $1.8 billion, while the annual subsidy in the guaranteed loan program is approximately $9.5 billion.[17]

The kinds of programs just discussed are appealing to politicians in part precisely because they are *not* readily apparent in the budget. Of course, any time an elected official can provide a benefit to a group and impose the cost in ways that are not obvious, he or she will be tempted to do just that. The *opportunity* to configure programs this way, of course, leads to further increases in the size of government because it reduces the *perceived* cost of government. Moreover, to the extent that public debate highlights concern over the deficit,

---

[17] *Budget of the United States Government, Fiscal Year 1991*, pp. 245 and 246.

Figure 21:   Federal Credit Programs, 1989

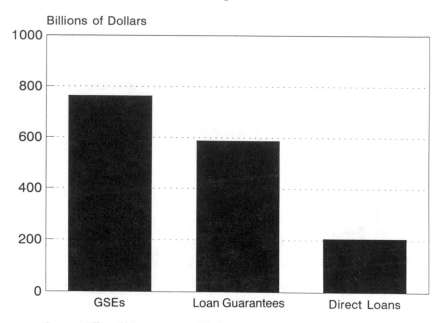

Billions of Dollars

SOURCE: Office of Management and Budget

and as the Gramm-Rudman-Hollings law imposes explicit strictures on deficit finance, one would expect an increasing tendency to finance programs either off budget or through using budget tricks to hide the real costs of programs.

A related issue is the major alternative way the government has of affecting resource allocation—regulation. Basically, the government can obtain command over resources in four ways: taxing and spending (with which we are all familiar), borrowing and spending (again, with which we are familiar), inflating (that is, simply printing the money—something that, fortunately, isn't practiced very frequently), and conscripting. *Direct* conscription of resources has been ruled unconstitutional except in the two key areas of jury duty and military service. But as the federal government endeavors to hold spending within bounds, it will feed its appetite for expanded dominion by indirect conscription—ordering the private sector to provide the resources.[18]

---

[18] Economists sometimes refer to such schemes as an implicit tax. On the general proposition of government's use of tools to obtain command over resources, see Robert W. Hahn, "Instrument Choice, Political Reform and Economic Welfare," *Public Choice* (1990): 243–56.

For example, the federal government could provide a system of child care centers throughout the nation. But this costs money. Thus, the government mandates that companies provide child care facilities for their employees. Another example: the federal government could clean up a polluted estuary on its own, or it may order companies along the estuary (some of whom may have had little to do with the pollution) to accomplish that task. Again, as demands for new programs increase, as opposition to tax increases mounts, and as there is greater public sensitivity to deficit finance, elected officials can be expected to increase the use of regulation. And because the costs of regulation tend to be hidden, the public will know even less about the federal government's true budget.

Myths about the budget

The second major reason for the failure of the U. S. budget is the uncritical acceptance of fashionable myths about the budget that receive currency primarily because belief in them leads to policies in accord with the proponents' own ideologies. No list of budget myths could be altogether inclusive—there are too many of them. But some of the more important ones are as follows.

Perhaps the most pernicious myth about the budget is the notion that tax increases are necessary to reduce the deficit. As a general proposition, tax rate increases slow down the economy because of the adverse effects on incentives. This major theme of supply side economics is not seriously contested by contemporary economists.[19] Also, as a general proposition, the ultimate effect on government revenue of a tax rate increase is indeterminate.[20] Depending on the item whose tax rate is increased and the time period under consideration,[21] a tax rate increase can either increase or decrease government revenue.

The above considerations aside, would an increase in government revenue—if there is one—actually be used to reduce the deficit? As we saw at the end of the previous chapter, a tax increase was put in place for 1988 and 1989, but the deficit actually increased (after coming down the previous year). In contrast, there have been instances of tax increases followed by progress in reducing the deficit. Several economists have looked at this question analytically and concluded that,

---

[19] The severity of the effect on the economy will depend on the specific taxes whose rates are increased.

[20] A few of the more extreme supply-siders have promoted the proposition that a tax rate increase will always *reduce* government receipts, but this notion has little currency among contemporary economists.

[21] Because incentives affect behavior over time, a tax rate increase usually has a greater revenue-enhancing effect in the short term than in the long term.

in the main, the federal government tends to spend increased revenues rather than using them to reduce the deficit.[22]

Recently, with the aid of George Mason University graduate students Tony Caporale and Gary Richardson, I used data from the past fifty years to address the following question: which is more effective in reducing the deficit—a reduction (or slowdown in the rate of increase) in spending or an increase in rates?[23] The results implied that spending cuts translated into a significant reduction of the deficit but that tax rate increases had only the most modest effect on the deficit.[24] From this and the research cited earlier, it appears that Congress tends to view total revenue (including a tolerable level of borrowing) as a simple spending limit; increase that sum and spending will be increased a like amount and vice versa. In short, progress on reducing the deficit is more likely to be made through efforts to restrain spending than through efforts to raise taxes.

A second, related myth about the budget is the notion that we as a nation are undertaxed. In fact, federal taxes are at record levels in both nominal and real (inflation-adjusted) terms. Moreover, as a proportion of gross national product, federal tax revenue remains at the plateau experienced over the past several decades (see figure 22). Another way of visualizing the tax burden is to think in terms of the time of year the typical individual completes working to pay taxes at all levels and starts working for himself. The Tax Foundation has been keeping records on what it calls "tax freedom day" for some time. In 1930, the magic date was February 15. In 1950, Americans worked for the government until April 3.

---

[22] See, for example, Richard Vedder, Lowell Gallaway, and Christopher Frenze, *Federal Tax Increases and the Budget Deficit, 1947–1986: Some Empirical Evidence* (prepared for the Congressional Joint Economic Committee), reprinted in 133 *Congressional Record*, April 30, 1987, pp. S-5754–55; William Anderson, Myles S. Wallace, and John T. Warner, "Government Spending and Taxation: What Causes What?" *Southern Economic Journal*, January 1986, pp. 630–39; Neela Manage and Michael L. Marlow, "The Causal Relationship between Federal Expenditures and Receipts," *Southern Economic Journal*, January 1986, pp. 617–29; and Rati Ram, "Additional Evidence on Causality between Government Revenue and Government Expenditure," *Southern Economic Journal*, January 1988, pp. 763–69.

[23] This simple multivariate (statistical) analysis had as its dependent variable the real (inflation-adjusted) deficit and as independent variables (a) various measures of outlay changes and (b) various measures of changes in tax rates.

[24] Many people—including some members of Congress—believe that a tax increase could be fashioned so that the increased revenues could be held in trust, assuring they would be used to reduce the deficit. The problem is, the deficit, by definition, is simply the difference between tax receipts and outlays. There is no way to treat one source of revenue differently from any other.

Figure 22: Federal Taxes as a Percent of Gross National Product

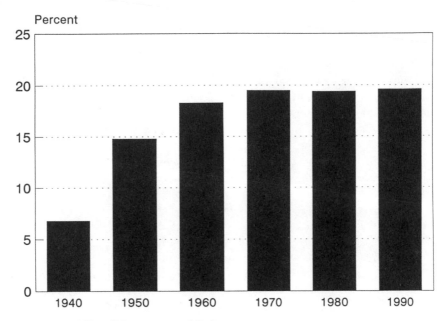

SOURCE: Office of Management and Budget

In 1970, tax freedom arrived on April 28. In 1990, the date was May 5—the latest ever.[25]

A third myth about the budget concerns the financing of spending. Whereas spending equals tax receipts plus borrowing, a complicating element is almost universally overlooked. When the federal government receives revenues from Medicare premiums, the sale of timber on federal lands, the sales to foreigners of surplus military equipment, and certain other transactions, these revenues enter the books technically as offsetting receipts, meaning that they show up on the books as negative outlays rather than as revenue. This treatment of such revenue is problematic for two reasons. First, it gives an erroneous picture of the true size of the federal government. For example, in 1990, total outlays were forecast by OMB to be $1,197.2 billion. However, this figure includes $36.5 billion in offsetting receipts. Thus, the true size of the spending side of the budget

---

[25] See Paul G. Merski, "May 5 Tax Freedom Day Is Latest Ever," Tax Foundation Special Report (April 1990), p. 1.

is more like $1,233.7 billion ($1,197.2 billion plus $36.5 billion). And the revenue side of the budget should receive a like adjustment.[26]

A second problem with offsetting receipts relates to the way they work. When each appropriations subcommittee is given its allocation under the budget resolution, it has to keep its funding within this limit. Almost always the subcommittee wishes to fund at a higher rate to expand its programmatic base. How to accomplish that? If the subcommittee can devise a way of generating revenue from the programs under its jurisdiction (for example, charging fees for the use of national parks, selling assets, or whatever), it may in effect use these offsetting receipts to fund expansions in its programs. In this way, individual appropriations subcommittees, working in tandem with their opposite number in the other House, can act as miniature Ways and Means/Finance committees—they can finance programs as well as fund them. Thus, there is an incentive for offsetting receipts to become an ever-increasing share of the federal budget and for the true size of the federal budget to become progressively understated.

A fourth myth about the budget is the notion that budget summits—involving the president and Congress—are productive in reducing the deficit. As we saw at the end of the previous chapter, this was certainly not the case for the 1987 summit, where the result was an *increase* in the deficit.

Such a retrogression on the deficit following a budget summit appears not to have been an aberration. A 1990 report by Paul G. Merski of the Tax Foundation finds that during the decade of the 1980s the deficit tended to *rise* following budget summits but to *fall* in years not covered by any budget agreement.[27] In all but one of the years covered by an agreement the deficit went up (see figure 23, adapted from Merski's report to include updated estimates for 1990 and 1991). In two of the four years in which there was *no* agreement the deficit went down (in particular, 1987); in the other two the deficit went up, but on balance the deficit went down. Knowing this tendency is one major reason I had so strongly opposed President Reagan's agreeing to the 1987 budget summit in the first place.

Moreover, bear in mind that in the era of Gramm-Rudman-Hollings, the true purposes of budget summits are (a) to *increase* the deficit and (b) to *reformulate* the means by which the deficit target is met. Take the 1990 summit as an example. Under the Gramm-Rudman-Hollings law, the forecast deficit for fiscal year 1991 could be no higher than $74 billion or else a sequester must be ordered to bring the deficit down to the $64 billion target. The budget summit was called when the severity of the sequester necessary to meet this deficit target was recognized.

---

[26] Ibid., pp. A-293 and A-294. Offsetting receipts in 1980 were $19.9 billion.

[27] See Paul G. Merski, "A Decade of Budget Summitry," Tax Foundation Issue Brief (May 1990), p. 1. Also, see his "Budget Deal Perpetuates Fiscal Failure," Tax Foundation Issue Brief (November 1991), p. 1.

Figure 23:   Changes in Federal Deficits, 1981–1990

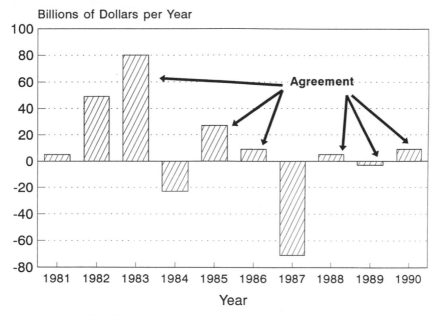

SOURCE: Office of Management and Budget

Although the discussion envisioned a major reduction in the deficit for 1991 (from a burgeoning current services level exceeding $200 billion), an implicit goal was to revise the Gramm-Rudman-Hollings target upward to something more "reasonable." Moreover, the discussion centered on meeting the deficit target through a combination of tax increases and spending restraints, not through spending restraints alone, as would be the case under a sequester.

A fifth myth about the budget is the notion that deficits are caused by overly optimistic revenue forecasting by the administration. The story goes something like this. In order to make the president's budget look good (that is, incorporate a low deficit), the administration pumps up its revenue forecast by making unduly optimistic assumptions about economic growth, inflation, total employment, and so forth. Then Congress, relying on these estimates, enacts spending measures that would result in a reasonable deficit *provided* the revenues materialize as promised by the administration. Of course they don't, and that's the reason the deficit is so high.

Each year I was responsible for the budget (covering fiscal years 1987-1989), I was on the receiving end of this charge from some members of Congress and

Figure 24:   Forecast versus Actual Deficits, 1987–1989

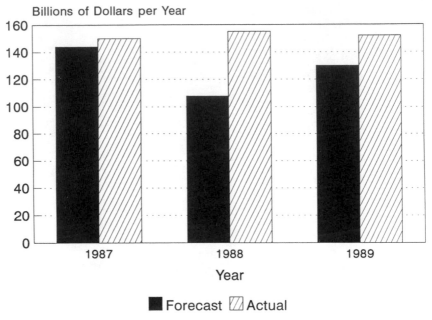

Billions of Dollars per Year

SOURCE: Office of Management and Budget

many in the media. Although it is true that the deficit turned out higher than we had forecast (see figure 24), the administration's revenue forecasts for the three years 1987–1989 were right on the mark (see figure 25).[28] However, we did underestimate outlays, especially in 1988 and 1989 (see figure 26), mainly because our forecasts were based on spending restraint measures the president advocated in his budgets but Congress refused to adopt.

A sixth myth about the budget is the notion that during the 1980s there was a radical transformation in the budget: an enormous *increase* in defense spending and a *reduction* in spending on human needs.

Although spending on defense did increase substantially during the decade,

---

[28] Tax reform, enacted after the 1987 forecasts were made, added a minor amount to 1987 revenue but not enough to change the basic story. Although the forecast for 1988 reflected the effects of tax reform, the later budget summit agreement added approximately $11 billion to revenue. The forecast for 1989, however, incorporated changes from both tax reform and the agreement.

Figure 25:   Forecast versus Actual Revenues, 1987–1989

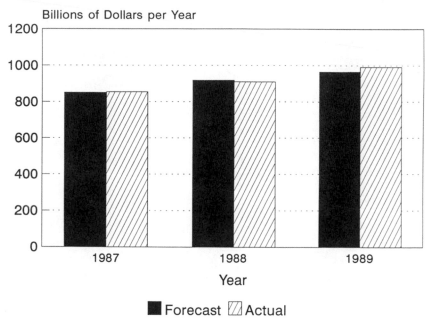

Billions of Dollars per Year

Year

■ Forecast ▨ Actual

SOURCE: Office of Management and Budget

so too did spending on programs such as Social Security, health, education, and others that, by convention, are categorized as "human resources." The actual increase in spending on human resources was much greater than the actual increase in spending on defense (see figure 27). In proportionate terms, however, the increase in defense spending was larger, though not nearly as large as the increase in interest on the debt. In all, the data undercut the notion that the defense buildup of the 1980s was financed by cuts in programs serving human needs. In fact, both categories of programs grew remarkably during the decade.

A seventh myth about the budget is the tendency to equate program spending with program effectiveness. This is particularly vexing for those who would tailor federal programs from the standpoint of cost-effectiveness, for whenever there is a new problem to address (for example, illicit drugs, long-term care for the elderly, or a drought), there is a run to the "highest common denominator." That is, whoever is in favor of spending the largest sum captures the public's attention as being the most serious and committed to solving the problem. The unleashing of a bidding war almost inevitably leads to wasteful spending. Not only is more

Figure 26:   Forecast versus Actual Outlays, 1987–1989

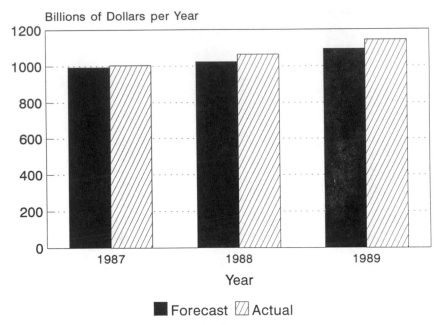

SOURCE: Office of Management and Budget

money appropriated than can be spent wisely but the composition of that spending is seldom consistent with a coherent and effective approach to the problem.[29]

At times bidding wars can approach the ridiculous. For example, in the summer of 1987 the Reagan administration negotiated at great length with Congress over reauthorization of housing legislation. At issue was whether the allowed annual appropriation for this program would be $12 billion, as the president recommended, or in excess of $20 billion, as many in Congress demanded. What was foolish about the rhetoric of many in Congress was that the housing program was already bursting at its seams, having an extremely large volume of unexpended budget authority in the pipeline. In fact, we at OMB estimated that should the program receive *zero* appropriations (zero budget authority) for the next several years, actual program spending (budget outlays) would continue to rise.

---

[29] Not only do most such approaches suffer from haste and a lack of coordination, but individual members of Congress often use must legislation of this sort to incorporate and thereby obtain passage of special-interest programs of their own.

Figure 27:   Composition of Federal Spending

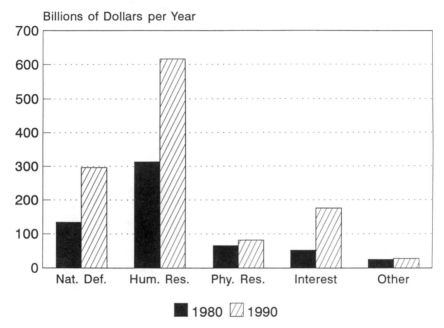

Billions of Dollars per Year

■ 1980   ▨ 1990

SOURCE: Office of Management and Budget

There are other myths about the budget. One is the notion that the national debt is owned by foreigners. Although the absolute amount of the debt held in foreign hands increased during the 1980s, the *proportion* of debt held by foreigners remained fairly constant—around 18 percent.[30] Another myth is that interest expense is overwhelming the budget. Although interest expense has risen dramatically in recent years, the current situation is not unprecedented; following World War II (when, for a brief time, borrowing exceeded tax receipts), net interest held a like command over total outlays.[31]

A particularly disabling myth about the budget is the incredible misinformation about Social Security. First, most elected representatives as well as the public at large do not realize that the program's benefits, on average, constitute

---

[30] *Budget of the United States Government, Fiscal Year 1991*, p. A-97.

[31] Ibid., p. A-304. It is also notable that the national debt exceeded the gross national product through the period 1944 through 1948, whereas it is just over half the gross national product today.

far more than an annuity one would be able to purchase with what they've paid
into the system, even counting interest. Second, the elderly as a class are not
poor; they are far better off than the young people who are paying the taxes that
go to finance Social Security benefits.

Institutional deficiencies

The major evidences of budget failure—chronic deficits, growing tax burdens,
and excessive spending—are themselves *symptoms* of an inefficient and incom-
plete set of budget institutions. The maturing subdiscipline known as public
choice illuminates the role that institutions play in the outcomes of collective
decision making, including the decisions rendered by the president and members
of Congress. The domain of public choice is the allocation of resources where
decisions are made collectively (by governments, in particular). Just as conventional economists study how private individuals and other single entities (such as
firms) make decisions to allocate resources in private markets, public choice
economists examine the process of resource allocation in a collective, or public
choice, framework. Just as conventional economists theorize that in private
markets incentives affect behavior (for example, lowering the price will lead to
an increase in unit sales as long as supplies remain available), public choice
economists theorize that incentives facing public decision makers will affect their
behavior. More important, they theorize that *changing* those incentives (more
particularly the institutions that provide those incentives) will lead to different
outcomes.

In this spirit Professor Mark Crain of George Mason University and I ex-
amined the institutional arrangements by which states go about their budgeting
and what this might say for federal budget making.[32] We noted at the outset that
the fifty states, which collectively spend a little less than half what the U.S.
government spends, presently run a healthy surplus and tend to complete their
budgets on time, with more attention to priorities. When we analyzed the data
carefully, we found there were good reasons for this difference in performance—
reasons that appear to go a long way in explaining the failure of our federal budget
system.

State governments, of course, are different from the federal government in
being much smaller and having a more limited scope (for example, no direct
equivalent to the national defense function). However, budget making at the state

---

[32] A summary of our work is found in W. Mark Crain and James C. Miller III, "Budget
Process and Spending Growth," *William and Mary Law Review*, Spring 1990, pp. 1021–
46. This section draws heavily on that work.

level is subject to the same kinds of influences experienced by legislators and the chief executive at the federal level. Our basic methodology was to utilize the conventional statistical technique of multivariate regression analysis to determine the effectiveness of various institutional arrangements. Specifically, we hypothesized that certain budget procedures would affect the outcomes and that by combining the data from all the states, we could statistically determine the effect of each of these factors on the growth of state spending.

As in the case of federal budgeting, state budgets become law after passage by the legislature and approval of the executive (or having her or his objection overridden). We first hypothesized that increasing the number of budget bills would reduce the rate of growth in spending because the larger the budget bill (that is, the smaller the number of total bills) the greater the value that accrues to the approving legislator and chief executive and the lower the relative cost to both. All can take credit for the benefits the measure contains, and all can blame others for its costs. About half the states budget by means of an omnibus appropriations measure, but the rest sometimes go to extraordinary lengths to divide the budget into separate bills—the average being thirty. Thus, we'd expect the rate of growth of government to increase as the average number of budget bills declines.

Second, Professor Crain and I hypothesized that the greater the specificity of the budget document, the greater would be the growth of spending. That is, the greater the control the legislators are allowed to exercise over the budget, the greater their incentive to see it expand. Everything else being equal, the greater the extent of micromanaging, the more rapid the growth of spending.

Third, we looked at the extent to which spending had to be appropriated for each budget cycle. Twenty-one states require that *all* spending be appropriated in each budget cycle, whereas the rest, like the federal government, have some spending programs imbedded in permanent law—that is, entitlements. Because it would seem that passage of an entitlement program raises the ante for the beneficiaries of that program more than the ante for those bearing the costs, we hypothesized that increasing the proportion of the state budget that is incorporated in permanent law would increase spending growth.

Fourth, we recognized that a major difference between state governments and the federal government is that most state governments require their budgets to be balanced. However, they differ as to whether this requirement is part of the state constitution or merely a requirement of the state legal code. Everything else being equal, we anticipated that a *constitutional* requirement would be a more effective brake on the growth of spending than a legislative requirement.

Receiving almost as much public attention as the balanced budget requirement is the authority that forty-four state governors have to line-item veto spending in their budgets. Our hypothesis was that the availability of the line-item veto would reduce the growth of spending. However, we were aware that some previous research had questioned whether, in fact, this was the case.[33] We also brought to our analysis knowledge that the state item vetoes differ in a small detail but one that makes a whale of a difference: In ten states the governor can not only eliminate a spending item from the budget but may reduce the amount appropriated.

Why is this important? Imagine a chief executive examining a remedial reading program funded at $5 million. Suppose he or she knows that in this particular year only $3 million in funds could be productively employed in this program. Is the governor going to accept the $5 million spending program or zero out the program altogether? Almost invariably the chief executive will choose to retain a sensitive program at its appropriated level rather than veto it and incur the political flack. *However*, if the chief executive has the power to reach in and strike out $5 million and replace it with $3 million (or even $4 million), this phenomenon, compounded over an entire budget, could lead to substantial savings. Thus, we hypothesized that the item-reduction veto would be most effective in restraining the growth of spending.

Lastly, we noted that in approximately one-third of the states the legislature as well as the executive prepares a budget. We found this of interest, in part because Congress is increasingly moving in that direction: after the president proposes his budget, the congressional leadership promptly proposes its counter-budget or at least a semblance of one. Because the executive's budget formulation is much more complete and constitutes the approach of analyzing each program on its merits, we hypothesized that the dual budget preparation would increase the rate of spending growth.

When Professor Crain and I completed our statistical analyses, we found that several institutional arrangements had significant effects on the growth of state spending. In particular, the powerful effect of the item-reduction veto consistently restrained the growth of spending. Likewise, a significant effect was associated with the budget bill format—the extent of control legislators have over its implementation: the more control, the greater the growth in spending. Finally, of great significance was the extent of nonappropriated funds in the budget—that is, the extent to which certain spending is automatic, part of permanent law. Predictably, the greater the proportion of entitlements, the greater the growth of spending.

Of lesser significance, we found, was that increasing the number of separate budget bills tended to reduce the rate of growth of spending, as did the consti-

---

[33] See, for example, Advisory Commission on Intergovernmental Regulations, "Significant Features of Fiscal Federalism" (1986); and Douglas Holtz-Eakin, "The Line-Item Veto and Public Sector Budgets: Evidence from the States," National Bureau of Economic Research (March 1988).

tutional balanced budget requirement. We also found that having a separate legislative budget tended to increase the rate of spending.

Although extrapolating these results based on state data to the possible effects on the federal budget is not easy, doing so helps gain some indication of the magnitudes involved. Specifically, if the item-reduction veto at the federal level were to have the same impact as we found it to have at the state level, then, had it been in effect in 1980, approximately half a *trillion* dollars would have been saved during the decade, or nearly $2,000 for each man, woman, and child in the country. On the whole, other institutional reforms would yield less significant effects, but their potential is dramatic nonetheless.

Of course, there are deficiencies in the U.S. budget system that have no direct analogues in state government. For example, the budget resolution passed by Congress is not a law but merely an agreement between the two Houses. Because the budget resolution is Congress's first major action on the budget, the leadership usually entices the president to negotiate its particulars. Yet there is no assurance that after such negotiations Congress will keep its side of the bargain. For years, President Reagan compromised over the budget resolution, agreeing to reductions in his request for defense and to an increase in domestic spending, only to see Congress in the end cut even more from defense and further augment domestic spending. Negotiations seldom work when one side repeatedly fails to deliver what is promised.

The House of Representatives in particular is characterized by process deficiencies that lead to budget failure. For example, there is no supermajority requirement for violating the Gramm-Rudman-Hollings deficit restraint. In the Senate, if a proposal arises that would increase spending or reduce revenue sufficient to raise the deficit above the Gramm-Rudman-Hollings target, that initiative is subject to a point of order requiring a three-fifths affirmative vote.[34] In the House, however, little more than lip service is paid to the statutory requirement for offsets[35] to be identified whenever an item is considered that would push the deficit above the target. The consequent lack of discipline, coupled with the absence of any threat of a sequester once the OMB director's report of October 15 has been issued, leads to a constant ratcheting up of the deficit during the legislative session.

Another deficiency is that the budget resolution specifies limits on budget authority *and* budget outlays for the Senate but limits budget authority *only* for

---

[34] In recent years this requirement in the Senate has been rendered less effective by the expedient of having the Senate vote on whether, in fact, the item deserves a point of order (such vote requiring a bare majority).

[35] For example, a proposal to increase spending on one program might be offset by a proposal to decrease spending a like amount in another area.

the House of Representatives. By artfully manipulating budget authority among accounts, the appropriations subcommittees in the House can dramatically increase outlays for favored programs.

Another budget game practiced by the appropriators is underfunding sensitive programs. It works like this. As a deliberate policy, the appropriators fund programs like food stamps and veterans' medical benefits at about 80 percent of the rate that is likely to be needed. This, of course, prompts the administration after the first of the year to ask for an emergency supplemental to which can be attached all manner of special-interest pork programs that will whisk through both Houses and past the president's desk as must legislation. In the meantime, this tactic has allowed the appropriators to fund other programs at levels higher than otherwise could be sustained.

A final institutional deficiency is missed deadlines. Often the administration is late in submitting the budget to Congress. The budget committees are nearly always late in reporting out the budget resolution, and Congress is late in passing it. During the decade of the 1980s the requirement of the Budget and Accounting Act that Congress complete the full contingent of thirteen separate appropriations bills before the beginning of the fiscal year was honored only in the breech. Decision making on the various budget documents suffers incredibly from undue complexity and insufficient review time. Those voting in Congress and those advising the president seldom have much more than a cursory understanding of what those documents contain.

No rational person would allow the lack of truth, the myths, and the institutional deficiencies discussed above to govern their own personal budget making. Why, then, do we rely on such a scheme to develop a budget that affects us all and that exceeds the gross national product of all but three countries in the world?

11 | Fixing the U.S. Budget

DESPITE THE CRITICAL TONE of this book, I do believe the U.S. budget can be saved. Doing so will require a fundamental restructuring of the federal budgeting process. Incremental reforms will only buy time and not much of that. What has to happen is for people generally to become so fed up with the budget's failures that they demand—and get—substantive action.

The needed reforms would change the incentives facing the major budget decision makers. The basic budget problem is *not*, as some allege, that the budget takes an ever-increasing portion of the president's time and that of members of Congress. Nor is it that the president and the congressional leadership have different ideas about budget priorities. The basic problem is that our decision-making institutions impart a bias toward greater size and scope of government than people really want. Reforms are needed that give decision makers incentives to respond to the will of the governed.

Recommendations for procedural reform

Adopting the following recommendations would enhance the public's understanding of the budget and the budget process. The recommendations would lead to a more deliberate setting of budget priorities and tend to eliminate deficit finance through spending restraint rather than tax increases. In sum, they would encourage budget decision makers to be more responsive to the public.

To ensure truth in budgeting

1. Eliminate the statutory requirement that a current services budget be prepared, and direct OMB and the Congressional Budget Office to

prepare all budget materials comparing proposed spending and revenue with the previous year's levels. This would dramatically reduce the cacophony of voices in Washington around budget time—some complaining that a budget proposal would cut spending, others complaining that it would increase spending; some complaining that it would raise taxes, others claiming it would be revenue-deficient. The same metric for everyone would be one to which the person on the street could relate. More important, addressing the budget this way would tend to reduce the growth of spending and hold taxes in check.

2. Once the budget is balanced, pay off the national debt in installments over a twenty-five-year period (roughly a generation). For each year, the interest on the debt plus the debt-reduction installment should be approximately a constant portion of total spending. Like a home mortgage, the principal would constitute a small portion of the payment in the initial years but would rise substantially toward the end of the payoff period. Making a commitment of this sort would not only relieve future generations of the debt overhang but would increase the efficiency of the economy.

3. Instruct the trustees to invest the Social Security surplus in something other than federal government securities. (Possibilities include state and local debt, limited commercial debt,[1] and real estate.) This would immediately halt the current practice of having the Social Security trust fund finance government spending. It would also mean that when the surplus is needed in the twenty-first century, there will be real assets to call on to finance benefits for baby boomers.

4. Begin raising Medicare premiums to cover the shortfall in Medicare's hospital insurance trust fund. This program will be a major drain on future generations if it is not put in sound fiscal condition now. Premiums presently cover 25 percent of the cost. Raising this to 35 percent or even 50 percent would not be unreasonable, given the incomes of most elderly.

5. Privatize the deposit insurance at financial institutions. The savings and loan debacle should have brought home the fundamental flaw in our system of government deposit insurance: it is incapable of deterring excessively risky undertakings. In private markets, premiums differentiate among risks and thereby *control* risks. For example, knowing that a history of automobile accidents and arrests for drunk driving will raise your insurance premium puts a damper on these activities for most people. For those who persist, companies will not insure them at any price. Private deposit insurance would work the same way—raising costs to institutions that increase

---

[1] Any investment in companies should be limited to debt (not equity) and only a minority portion of that to avoid problems attendant with government ownership.

the riskiness of their portfolios and cutting off those that fail to heed warnings. Just as states require that cars be insured to meet certain minimal standards, the federal government could require financial institutions to carry deposit insurance. The result would be a more efficient system of insurance, more efficiently operating financial markets, and an end to this enormous taxpayer liability.

6. Implement a comprehensive program of credit reform by selling loan portfolios to the private sector and obtaining insurance for loan guarantees from private markets. Assuming that the federal government's credit programs cannot be eliminated, they ought to be treated more efficiently in the budget. At present, agencies have strong incentives to make loans and weak incentives to collect them. Actual loans are recorded in the budget as outlays; repayments are recorded as offsetting receipts. If these loan assets (promissory notes) were sold to the private sector, the programs' administrators would have greater incentive to keep track of loans due and to take more seriously the screening of applicants. This would improve the repayment record and lower the taxpayer subsidy. Also, by recording as outlays the difference between the face value of the loans and the amount received upon sale, the amount of the subsidy would be revealed and priorities within the program could be more readily evaluated.

Incentives would work in a similar fashion if private insurance had to be obtained to back federal loan guarantees. At present, loan defaults are not the responsibility of current program administrators, who are now only interested in making new commitments. By bringing the cost of the loan guarantee to bear directly on the official making the guarantee, an increase in the quality of loan guarantees would be forthcoming, as would a consequent reduction in defaults. Moreover, the actual subsidy would be revealed in the form of the insurance premium paid, making it easier to evaluate the program. Both reforms would reduce the federal government's role in credit markets and reduce taxpayer subsidies.

7. Compile a regulatory budget and set yearly limits. To provide more discipline in the regulatory process and to limit the ability of Congress to finance programs by means of indirect conscription, the president should compile a budget estimating the costs imposed by major regulatory programs that are expected to operate during the year. Congress should review this budget, and by means of a joint resolution (that is, a law) the president and Congress should agree on a limit.[2]

---

[2] This is not to imply there would be an absence of debate over the appropriate methodology for estimating regulatory costs. However, the Office of Information and Regulatory Affairs in OMB is quite capable of providing an initial report, which could then be the subject of review by the Congressional Budget Office and the committees in Congress.

To combat budget myths

1. Publish and disseminate data and analysis on changes in federal revenues and outlays. Each new budget should emphasize historical trends in government spending and finance. This would enable the general public to see the lack of any reliable relationship between tax increases and reductions in the deficit.

2. Publish and disseminate data and analyses on the extent of federal taxes and their impact on the economy. People need to view taxes in a historical perspective and understand that tax rate increases tend to slow economic growth.

3. Report the budget in a format that shows offsetting receipts as additions to both outlays and revenues and channel those receipts directly into the Treasury. The appropriate measure of the size of government includes offsetting receipts on the revenue side of the ledger, not as a deduction from outlays. Because offsetting receipts are a growing part of the budget, exposing them would draw people's attention to the escalating size and scope of government. Also, channeling all offsetting receipts directly into the Treasury would take away from the appropriations sub-committees the ability to use them to finance increased spending. This would tend to reduce total outlays.

4. Disavow budget summits as a way of solving the deficit problem. As we have seen, budget summits tend to *increase* the deficit, not reduce it. If the president and members of Congress were to resolve to formulate the budget through the conventional legislative process, the result would be greater progress on the deficit and a greater check on the growth of government.

5. Publish and highlight the relationship between budget forecasts and actual performance. The data show that revenue increases tend to materialize, whereas actual outlays tend to run above forecast levels. The implication that budget decision makers tend to ratchet spending upward and that this is a major reason for poor performance in reducing the deficit would not be lost on the American people.

6. Detail and emphasize changes in spending levels for major components of the budget and changes in the budget's composition. This would undercut claims by some bent on increasing total spending that given budget proposals constitute an abandonment of traditional responsibilities to meet human needs. During the past decade social programs have grown sizably, remaining a large fraction of total expenditures.

7. Publish and disseminate more analyses of the effectiveness of specific programs, especially programs that were enacted on short notice. Something has to dissuade people—including budget decision makers—of

the notion that total funding is an adequate measure of the effectiveness of a program. In many cases, additional funding can be counterproductive. Also, in most cases programs can be made more cost-effective through changes in the program's structure. Knowing this would prompt taxpayers to demand more accountability from program supporters and make them less tolerant of wasteful spending.

8. Focus public attention on other budget myths. In particular, point out the nature of the national debt, by whom it is held, and the relationship between Social Security benefits and amounts paid in. Budget policy is likely to be better if the facts are clearly understood.

To *reform the institutions*

1. Promulgate a constitutional amendment giving the president an item-reduction veto. Although many members of Congress strongly oppose giving the president additional powers over the budget, it is essential that an item-reduction amendment be placed before state legislatures as soon as possible. The importance of this institutional change in restraining the growth of the federal government cannot be overemphasized.

2. Greatly reduce the amount of specificity in the budget. Congress should endeavor to at least *halve* the number of line-item appropriations. In addition, the president should exert his constitutional authority so that money is not spent on specific items enumerated in appropriations committee reports that do not appear in the legislation. A reduction in the extent of congressional micromanaging of the federal budget would relieve pressure for expanding the size and scope of government.

3. Sunset entitlement programs and require that they be enacted each year. More than half the budget (excluding interest on the debt) now consists of spending programs embodied in permanent law. Scrutiny of these programs is nowhere near as close as of programs that are appropriated annually. In fact, these programs are frequently referred to as *uncontrollables*, implying that they cannot be changed. In fact, they can be changed, as they often are. But having to pass an annual review and appropriation would enhance program effectiveness and reduce waste.

4. Promulgate a constitutional amendment to require a balanced budget and a supermajority to increase taxes. The budget is unlikely to be balanced unless a specific requirement is put in the constitution. Also, to keep this requirement from becoming an excuse to raise taxes, a three-fifths vote of Congress should be required to raise any tax rates or to expand the tax base. This requirement should become effective several years out, however, to allow for a gradual reduction of the deficit (as envisioned in

various versions of Gramm-Rudman-Hollings as well as the 1990 budget deal—that is, the Omnibus Budget Reconciliation Act of 1990).

5. Convert the budget resolution into a budget law. There is good reason for the president and Congress to agree on the dimensions of the budget as incorporated in the budget resolution passed each spring. However, to make the resolution binding (and thus properly subject to negotiations), it must have teeth. Converting the present concurrent resolution into a joint resolution would accomplish that.

6. Revise the Budget and Accounting Act to require full funding of sensitive programs. Under the 1990 budget deal, any presidential requests for emergency appropriations are exempt from the ceilings on spending.[3] A way of assuring there will be such requests (and thus increases in total spending) is for Congress to underfund sensitive programs. The budget act should be amended to force the appropriators to include reasonable funding for such programs in ordinary appropriations.

7. Provide pay incentives for officials of the legislature and the executive to meet the timetables of the budget process. Although this may sound radical, especially to the relevant officials, it is an approach that will work: during any period the president's budget is late, the president, the vice-president, and the president's cabinet should receive half their usual pay. During any period that Congress misses its deadlines (budget resolution, appropriations, and reconciliation), its members should receive half their usual pay. And during any period the budget process goes over into the new fiscal year, *both* the executive (the president, the vice-president, and members of the cabinet) and members of Congress should receive half their usual pay. In one fell swoop, this would all but eliminate missed deadlines.[4]

Suggestions for a leaner, meaner budget

A major thesis of this book has been the need to eliminate the deficit through restraints on spending rather than increases in taxes. But just how do you restrain spending? Below I offer some concrete suggestions.[5] These suggestions will not

---

[3] See the Appendix.

[4] When I offered this solution to a budget committee chairman one day, he responded that the idea of financial incentives had merit but suggested instead that officials be given a *bonus* if they completed the budget process on time.

[5] There is no dearth of suggestions for ways to restrain spending. The president's budget each year contains many proposals, as do the debates over the budget resolution, appropriations, and reconciliation. In addition, each year the Congressional Budget Office puts

all be popular, nor will elected officials rush to embrace them. To solve our budget deficit problem means setting priorities and making hard choices—funding those programs that are most important and delaying others or eliminating them altogether. Let us take major categories of spending one at a time, starting with defense.

  1. *Defense:* 1992 base—$299 billion. There are some significant opportunities for savings on defense, though not as much as many peace dividend advocates allege.[6] First, Pentagon funding should be put on a multiyear basis. Because of long lead times for weapons systems, commitments must be made and adhered to. The uncertainties and erratic funding caused by the present system of yo-yo budgeting add tremendous costs to Pentagon procurement. Variations and delays in orders limit the potential savings from orderly production. Uncertainties created by a fickle Congress are treated like ordinary risks, with the costs passed through to the taxpayer. Conservatively, the defense budget could be lowered $10 billion a year without any reduction in readiness through multiyear, stable budgeting.

  Second, we need to improve our procurement system—make it more competitive and less laden with red tape. Although improvements have been made in recent years, there remains altogether too much sole-source contracting in the military, which escalates costs. Moreover, in a well-intentioned but overly zealous effort to maintain quality, the military has promulgated exacting specifications for everything from chairs to chocolate chip cookies. In many cases, off-the-shelf goods would serve just as well at much lower cost than the special orders meeting the military's particular specifications. Some procurement reforms require legislation; others require action by hidebound bureaucrats. An increase in the competitive provision of goods, plus a modicum of flexibility (and increased account-

---

out a compendium of options (see, for example, *Reducing the Deficit: Spending and Revenue Options*, 1990 Annual Report [February 1990]), and the Heritage Foundation occasionally publishes a specific proposal (see, for example, *Slashing the Deficit, Fiscal Year 1990* [1989]).

[6] Aside from the mobilization in the Persian Gulf, there is little evidence the world is a *safer* place today than before the great upheaval in Eastern Europe. As of yet, the Soviet Union has not *reduced* its ability to wage war; indeed, it has continued to modernize its armed forces. The incredible reforms in Eastern Europe—enabled by a strong U.S. defense posture throughout the 1980s—hold the *potential* for a significant lessening of tensions and substantial *multilateral* disarmament. Until that time, however, we would be wise to maintain our defenses at roughly their current levels, and thus the suggestions above go to savings in roughly the current force configuration.

ability) afforded procurement officers could lead to billions of dollars annually in additional savings.

Finally, we must do something about the propensity of members of Congress to use the defense budget as fodder for their reelection campaigns. Year after year, the military gets weapons systems they don't want and can't use. Why? Because they are made in some influential congressperson's district or senator's state. We maintain obsolete bases throughout the United States for the same reason: proposals to close them incur the wrath of the powerful. There are billions of dollars a year wasted here.

2. *Social Security:* 1992 base—$288 billion. Although our political leaders are extraordinarily reluctant to even utter the words Social Security unless in the context of defending the system, there is good reason to reform the program in a way that will reduce outlays. Recognizing that the vast majority of Social Security benefits are not earned but reflect the Ponzi nature of the program, benefits in excess of contributions should be based on need. Probably the best way to accomplish this further[7] means testing of excess Social Security benefits is to use the tax system. A good start would be to tax excess benefits as ordinary income, as is the case with a pension program.[8] As an exception to the proposed treatment of offsetting receipts described above, these receipts should be treated as a deduction in Social Security costs rather than as an increase in revenue. This change in Social Security benefits should reduce Social Security outlays by something on the order of 10 percent—about $29 billion.[9]

3. *Other Entitlement Programs:* 1993 base—$360 billion. Despite the rhetoric—that President Reagan tried to "balance the budget on the backs of Medicare patients"—Medicare spending more than doubled during the 1980s and for 1992 exceeded $116 billion.[10] The problem is not merely that there are more elderly to care for but that Medicare is a third-party

---

[7] Social Security benefits are already means tested to a limited extent. That portion of Social Security benefits that pushes the taxable income of a single person over $25,000 per year and a married couple over $32,000 per year is taxed as ordinary income.

[8] Treating Social Security in the same way as a pension fund would level the playing field and increase the likelihood of implementing more efficient private alternatives to Social Security, such as the proposal being advanced by Congressman John Porter.

[9] During the 1980s, the federal government of Australia brought its spending down from 29 percent of gross domestic product to 24 percent, in part by means testing their Social Security benefits.

[10] Medicare spending grew from $6.2 billion in 1970 to $32.1 billion in 1980. It is estimated to be $96.6 billion in 1990. *Budget of the United States Government, Fiscal Year 1991*, pp. A-293 and A-294.

payer; thus devices to keep payments to doctors and to hospitals within reason have achieved only modest success. Also, Congress has been quite willing during the past decade to *expand* the program's coverage to include elective procedures. A reform package that curtailed unreasonable expansions, that incorporated more creative and effective limits on provider compensation,[11] and that called for greater copayments and more second opinions (to limit excessive procedures) would save as much as $10 billion annually.

The farm program administered by the federal government is an abomination. Not only does it cost the public enormous sums, but by its design it perpetuates the problem and even makes it worse. Briefly, the program works like this: the government lends money to farmers on the assumption that they will receive a target price for their commodities (corn, wheat, rice, et cetera). If the market price rises above the target price, farmers take the market price and pay off the loan. But it usually doesn't happen that way (which is why the program exists, after all); in that case the farmer simply defaults on the loan, and the taxpayer picks up the difference.

What's wrong with that? First, the morality of it all: defaulting on loans is the accepted way of doing business with the government! Second, the amount of the subsidy (that is, the difference between the market price and the target price) in recent years has been more than the market price itself; this means that the taxpayer is paying farmers in these programs more than consumers of those commodities. Third, the stakes are high: for a farm population that makes up less than 5 percent of the total population (down from 16 percent in 1960), direct farm program outlays reached $26 billion in 1986 (though somewhat lower today). Finally, the real tragedy is that the program is so inefficient. Most subsidies go not to the small, struggling family farmer but to the multimillion-dollar outfits that are as good at farming the federal government as they are at farming the land. Also, the program perpetuates itself. Rather than providing a cushion to help marginal farmers make the transition into other commercial activities (as increasing productivity comes up against a fairly inelastic demand for foodstuffs), by establishing the target price so high, the program entices more farmers into business and marginal farmers to hang on despite the odds.

This program should be redesigned, first, to facilitate the adjustment

---

[11] In particular, it should be recognized that payment rates to hospitals by and large determine hospital capacity, in much the same way that price regulation by the old Civil Aeronautics Board determined airline capacity (load factors). In short, contrary to current practice, evidence that some hospitals are losing money should not be sufficient grounds for increasing compensation rates.

process toward a leaner agriculture sector; second, to direct support to the small family farmer rather than to the large agricultural enterprises; and third, to increase demand for U.S. agriculture by opening foreign markets to U.S. exports and reducing the subsidies afforded agriculture in countries that are our major competitors (but not by limiting agriculture imports or subsidizing U.S. exports). The objective should be to phase out this relic of the New Deal altogether and replace it with a more direct and efficient program of support for family farmers. The savings would exceed $10 billion per year.

Many other entitlement programs should be reformed. Tuition grants for higher education should be replaced by government loan guarantees.[12] Government direct and loan guarantee programs for commercial enterprises should be ended.[13] The savings potential is considerable.

4. *Domestic Appropriations:* 1992 base—$238 billion. Although domestic appropriated accounts diminished in real terms during the early 1980s, they have grown in real terms since,[14] and there is considerable room for the elimination of lower-priority programs. The pork programs mentioned in the last chapter are certainly a starting point. But almost every program could benefit from close scrutiny of its effectiveness, and on this basis many would be reduced in scope or eliminated entirely. For example, inefficient programs and agencies such as the Appalachian Regional Commission and the Interstate Commerce Commission should be abolished.

Also, there needs to be a serious commitment to productivity improvement. Just as companies rely on productivity increases to reduce cost and improve service delivery in the private sector, taxpayers should expect no less of government agencies. The potential savings are huge.

The federal government should shed those discretionary spending programs that might be undertaken more efficiently by the private sector. The private express statutes (giving the U.S. Postal Service a monopoly on first-class mail) should be repealed, and ownership of the postal service should be transferred in part to postal service employees and the rest offered for

---

[12] The market imperfection to be addressed is the relative impossibility of using one's human capital as collateral. The need for government is to provide that collateral, not to make outright tuition *grants*.

[13] In these cases there is no market imperfection: if a commercial operation has no collateral, the U.S. government has no business committing the U.S. taxpayer as lender or guarantor.

[14] See, for example, John F. Cogan and Timothy J. Muris, "Domestic Discretionary Spending in the 1980s," Hoover Institution Working Paper E-90-19 (July 1990).

public sale in the form of common stock. The billions of dollars in annual public subsidy to the postal service should be terminated. Amtrak should be sold to the highest bidder. This would result in a corridor rail service in the Northeast, probably one on the West Coast, and possibly a hub-and-spoke system centered in Chicago. In any event, its half-a-billion-dollar yearly subsidy should be ended.

The several Power Marketing Administrations should be sold. Nineteen out of twenty watts of power in this country are delivered by investor-owned companies, and they provide such service more efficiently than these U.S. government enterprises. The government interest subsidy should end, as well as the interest subsidy for rural electrical and telephone cooperatives. The U.S. Weather Service should be terminated, with private companies (such as Accu-Weather) allowed to take up the slack. And space exploration should be transferred gradually to the private sector, except, possibly, for defense and intelligence needs. These and other privatization initiatives would generate revenue (to ease the transition to zero deficits) as well as end a drain on the U.S. Treasury.

5. *Interest on the Debt:* 1992 base—$199 billion. Interest on the national debt, of course, is the product of the size of the debt and the average interest rate paid on government securities. Reducing the deficit would mean a smaller debt to service. Also, reducing the deficit would lower the average interest rate (although the full effect would take a while because the debt turns over slowly). The exact reduction in the interest rate paid by the federal government is difficult to estimate precisely, but even a reduction of a few tenths of a percent would mean savings of billions of dollars per year.[15]

Another way of reducing interest on the national debt would be to issue indexed bonds—that is, bonds whose principal and interest would be automatically adjusted for inflation. By removing a major source of uncertainty—inflation—the federal government would be able to secure funds at lower real interest expense. This has been tried and proven successful in Great Britain. Although such a move would be opposed by many on Wall Street and by officials at the Treasury Department, it should be implemented without delay. The potential savings are in the billions of dollars a year.

The spending restraint measures identified above are indicative of the alternatives available to reduce or eliminate the deficit without raising taxes. For some

---

[15] Reducing the deficit would not only lower federal interest expense but would lower the real rate of interest in private markets, thus enhancing economic growth.

of these measures, such as Medicare reforms, the initial savings would be large. But just as important there would be a "wedge effect"—that is, because of the initial savings the current services spending base would be lower in subsequent years. In short, taking initiatives such as these would mean recurring savings forever. Accordingly, it is eminently feasible to eliminate the deficit over a period of several years by restraining the growth of spending and relying on automatic revenue increases (through economic growth and so forth). In short, those in Washington who maintain that the deficit can't be reduced without raising taxes are making a political statement, not a technical statement. [16]

Postscript

With all the machinations over President Bush's "kinder and gentler" budget, summit negotiations, the 1990 budget deal, President Clinton's "vision," congressional reaction, and the 1993 budget deal, this writer is struck by a sense of déjà vu. The more things change, the more they stay the same. A president hypes his budget priorities; leaders of Congress go on the attack; the public is confused and befuddled; the press makes matters little better because of its own biases and failures to do its homework on budget details; and the "reality" is that the deficit can't be reduced unless taxes are increased. Yet, budget deals lead to increased deficits and larger government.

The major lesson of my recent experience with budgeting is that in terms of proper performance of government, the budget *process* is far more important than the budget *players*. That is, the incentives the players face and the set of constraints under which they operate are far more important determinants of what the budget looks like than who happens to be in Congress or the White House.

As my George Mason University colleague Dick Wagner points out, the basic problem is that with respect to budget making we have a "tragedy of the commons." [17] Just as competing sheepherders will overgraze common property, members of Congress will "overgraze" the budget. If a congressman can get a benefit for his district or state and have *all the people* pay for it, he will be compelled to do just that. And there are innumerable opportunities for members of Congress to behave in this manner. Consequently, there is burgeoning demand for government to expand. Every member of Congress sees the marginal benefits

---

[16] The CBO report (note 5, this chapter) contains spending reform options that would trim $96 billion from the CBO current services baseline for 1991. The Heritage report (note 5, this chapter) recommends a spending cut of $128 billion from the 1989 spending base.

[17] See Richard E. Wagner, "Grazing the Federal Budgetary Commons: The Rational Politics of Budgetary Irresponsibility," *Journal of Law & Politics*, Fall 1992, pp. 105–19.

Figure 28: Federal Deficits, 1984 to 1992

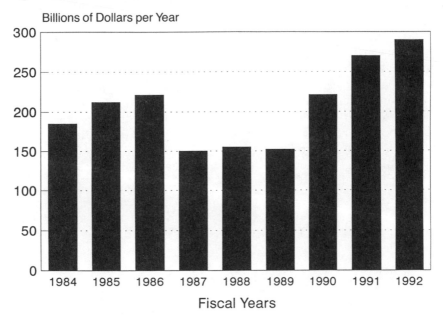

SOURCE: Office of Management and Budget

of increased spending greater than the costs, although from the standpoint of the *whole* Congress the benefits of new spending are *less* than the costs. Moreover, because the process resembles a riot more than a market, there is great inefficiency in resource allocation. This tragedy of the commons leads to a situation where the electorate demands limits on spending and more efficiency in priority setting but where our elected officials are incapable of responding because of powerful incentives.

The program outlined in the previous chapter would change incentives, but would it do the job? The evidence suggests it would. The only time in recent history when we had a substantial reform of this sort—the first year under Gramm-Rudman-Hollings—the deficit fell a record $71 billion. This was accomplished entirely on the spending side; there were no tax rate increases. Indeed, federal spending, adjusted for inflation, actually *fell* for the first time in two decades.

Further progress would have been made on the deficit through spending restraint had the president not been weakened because of Irangate and had there been no market crash, which served as a catalyst for the congressional leadership to justify a budget deal waiving the Gramm-Rudman-Hollings targets. But even without further progress, the deficit remained relatively low. When the Gramm-Rudman-Hollings targets were waived again, the deficit continued its upward path (see figure 28).

As Mark Crain and I have found, states that have the types of budget institutions advocated here have an easier time making ends meet and controlling the impulse to increase spending.

The very fact that most of the reforms advocated here are opposed so strongly by a majority of the members of Congress is testament to the likely effects of such reforms. Members of Congress like to spend money on their constituents and have someone else foot the bill, even if it means an increase in the deficit. This makes it easier for them to get reelected.

For the budget to be saved, the recommendations outlined above must be followed. Isn't it time we fixed the federal budget?

Appendix:
The U.S. Budget
and Budget Process
in Brief

THE FEDERAL BUDGET DETAILS AS WELL AS SUMMARIZES all the revenues and outlays of the federal government in a given year.[1] It is a *cash* budget. That is, revenues and outlays are counted in the year in which they occur.[2]

The federal budget is enormous. Revenues and outlays exceed $1 trillion. On average, the federal government spends more than $2.6 million every minute throughout the year. (A jet plane flying the speed of sound and reeling out dollar bills tied end to end would have to fly for 14.2 years to reel out $1 trillion.) According to the Tax Foundation, in 1990 the typical U.S. citizen had to work until March 23 just to pay his or her federal taxes (and until May 5 to pay state and local taxes).[3]

The federal government's revenue is derived almost exclusively from two categories: taxing and borrowing (that is, running a deficit).[4] The largest source of taxes is the personal income tax (see figure 29). A close second is run by receipts from the Social Security tax paid by employers and employees. Taxes on

---

[1] Thus, it is an *accounting* document. However, because almost everything the federal government does has implications for revenues or outlays, the budget is also a *policy* document.

[2] For example, a personal income tax liability from last year paid this year is counted as this year's income. A financial obligation by the federal government incurred this year but paid next year is counted as next year's expenditure.

[3] See Paul G. Merski, "May 5 Tax Freedom Day Is Latest Ever," Tax Foundation Special Report (April 1990), p. 1.

[4] The government also receives revenue from interest on deposits in financial institutions and occasionally from sales of assets (land, loan portfolios, and so forth). In particular, see the discussion in chapter 10 concerning the government's reliance on offsetting receipts.

Figure 29:   Sources of Federal Revenue, 1992

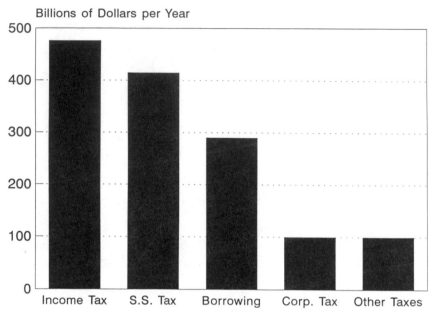

Billions of Dollars per Year

SOURCE: Office of Management and Budget

corporate income run third, followed by other taxes. Borrowing as a source of revenue exceeds corporate taxes but is less than the tax on Social Security.

Total spending can be viewed several ways; see figure 30 for a useful summary. As is often pointed out, interest on the national debt is the third largest expense, following human resources (of which Social Security and Medicare are the largest components) and national defense.

Another way of looking at spending is to distinguish between what are called *entitlements* and those programs that are appropriated each year. Entitlement programs—sometimes called *uncontrollables*—are spending commitments that are part of permanent law. That is, as long as Congress and the president do not change the law, a person or organization may be entitled to certain payments. Social Security, Medicare, and the farm subsidy program are all examples of entitlement programs; if you qualify under existing law, you are entitled to the payment. There is no cap on entitlement payments; if more people qualify than were expected, then spending must go up and vice versa. Entitlement spending accounted for $645 billion in 1992—more than half of all programmatic spending (that is, excluding interest on the debt).

Figure 30:   Categories of Spending, 1992

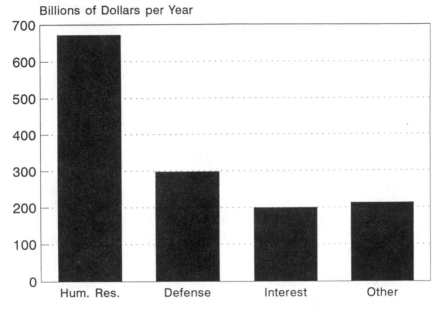

Billions of Dollars per Year

SOURCE: Office of Management and Budget

Budget years differ from ordinary calendar years. The budget year, called a *fiscal year*, begins on October 1 of the previous calendar year.[5] For example, the fiscal year for 1994 begins on October 1, 1993, and runs through September 30, 1994.

Preparation for a given year's budget begins long before the beginning of the fiscal year and sometimes doesn't end until after the new fiscal year has begun. The process usually gets under way in earnest two summers before the beginning of the fiscal year in question. For example, during the summer of calendar year 1994, work will begin on the fiscal year 1995 budget.

Briefly, there are three stages in the budget process. The first is the preparation of the budget the president *proposes* to Congress. This runs roughly from summer until the budget is submitted in January or February. The second stage is congressional deliberation and formulation of the budget, which the president signs. With luck, this process runs from January or February until the end of September,

---

[5] Until passage of the Budget and Accounting Act in 1974, the fiscal year began on July 1 of the previous calendar year.

but often it runs past September and even into December (after the fiscal year began on October 1). The third stage is determining whether spending restraints are required under the Omnibus Budget Reconciliation Act of 1993.

More specifically, the process works as follows. During the summer, the Office of Management and Budget (OMB) sends all agencies guidance, called a *mark*, indicating their spending limits and overall policies for the budget year under preparation. The aggregate of these marks, together with the forecast of government receipts, must lead to a projected deficit consistent with the 1993 act.

In September and October, the agencies respond with their proposed budgets. OMB reviews these budgets for conformance with their marks and with the president's overall policies. After revisions (reflecting staff-level discussions with the agencies), these proposals are aggregated into thirteen separate components (or *books*) for further analysis and changes at Director's Reviews, attended by the OMB analysts and other budget officials (as well as, occasionally, by members of the White House staff). After the OMB director's decisions, the revised budget proposals are aggregated into a single document for presentation to the president.

After the president has approved the OMB revised budget, ideally in late November but more usually in early December, the budgets are passed back (called the *passback*) to the agencies. The agencies then may appeal these changes to OMB and, if not satisfied, to the president (although sometimes there is an interim step: presentation to some sort of budget review board headed by senior White House officials).[6] After all decisions are final, OMB pulls the numbers together and prepares a final budget that is printed for the president to submit to Congress in January or February.[7]

Congressional deliberation begins immediately on receipt of the budget. (Usually, members of Congress are briefed on certain aspects of the budget before it is submitted by the president.) In both the House of Representatives and the Senate there are three committees with major jurisdiction over the budget. The budget committees in each House establish overall targets for spending (by major category) and for revenue (by major component). These targets must comport with the specifications established in the 1993 budget deal for the year in question. The Ways and Means Committee in the House and the Finance Committee in the Senate determine sources of tax revenue and spending on entitlement pro-

---

[6] The vast majority of appeals are resolved by discussions between the agencies and OMB. As a rule, few appeals go to the president.

[7] Two major budgets are not part of this review process: the budgets for the legislative branch (Congress) and the judicial branch (courts). In these cases, the president simply incorporates the budgets submitted to him by the congressional leadership and the administrator of the federal court system.

grams, such as Social Security and Medicare. Because both the tax code and the entitlement programs are permanent law, these two committees determine appropriate changes in those laws. Also, because entitlement spending is so large, these committees are responsible for more than half of all programmatic spending as well as all taxing. Finally, the Appropriation committees in both Houses, through their thirteen separate subcommittees, determine spending levels for individual agency programs (other than entitlement programs).

Although there is considerable simultaneous activity, in theory the budget committees first establish their overall parameters, to which the Ways and Means/ Finance and Appropriations committees respond. Under the Budget and Accounting Act, the budget committees must produce a budget resolution for consideration by the full House and Senate by April 1 of the year. Both Houses must then agree on a budget resolution by April 15.[8]

The Ways and Means/Finance and Appropriations committees then begin their work and produce bills for floor deliberation, ideally in ample time for final action before the end of the fiscal year. The work of the Ways and Means and Finance committees is called a *reconciliation* bill because it reflects adjustments in tax revenues and entitlement spending necessary to make the numbers work out, or reconcile, nonappropriations activities with the targets approved by Congress pursuant to the recommendations of the budget committees.

The work of the Appropriations committees ideally is reflected in thirteen separate appropriations bills but sometimes takes the form of a single omnibus appropriations measure or perhaps a few separate appropriations bills plus a catchall bill containing the remaining appropriations. To receive appropriations, a program or agency must be authorized, meaning that Congress establishes the program and usually sets a limit on the amount of money that may be appropriated each year. (Thus, negotiations over a program's or agency's funding level may occur at the point of authorization as well as in yearly appropriations.)[9] What Congress appropriates is called *budget authority*—permission and mandate to spend certain sums. Actual spending by agencies is called a *budget outlay*. In any given year, a program typically utilizes budget authority from previous years as well as the present year; moreover, some of the year's budget authority will be

---

[8] This is technically known as a *concurrent resolution*—an agreement between the two Houses of Congress. Ordinary laws are *joint resolutions*, which require the president's approval or override of the president's disapproval by a two-thirds vote of both Houses.

[9] Some programs and agencies are on a permanent authorization (for example, the Department of Defense). Others are authorized for fixed periods exceeding a year (for example, the National Endowment for the Arts). Still others require yearly authorization but, failing action by their authorizing committees, are authorized by means of a rider on their yearly appropriations bill (for example, the Federal Trade Commission).

held over until future years.[10] Budget authority is analogous to money put in a bank checking account; budget outlays are analogous to writing (and clearing) the checks.

Often the new fiscal year begins without Congress's having completed action on the budget. If the reconciliation bill hasn't passed, taxing and spending continue under the laws then in effect.[11] In the case of appropriations, Congress usually passes what it terms an *emergency continuing resolution*. Ideally, this is simply an extension of appropriations at rates in effect the previous year, but in practice the bill usually incorporates numerous increases for pet programs. In the event Congress doesn't pass an acceptable continuing resolution, the president is forced to close down government activities not appropriated (except for certain national security functions, which he is authorized to continue under the Constitution).

The end of this second stage of the budget process may be complicated by the third stage—a determination of whether spending reductions may be required under the 1993 act. Before the 1990 deal, on August 25 of each year, the OMB director issued an initial report saying whether the forecast deficit for the coming (fiscal) year exceeded the Gramm-Rudman-Hollings target for that year. If it exceeded this target by more than $10 billion (the margin of error incorporated in the legislation), the president issued an initial order sequestering enough spending resources (primarily budget authority) to bring the forecast deficit down to the Gramm-Rudman-Hollings target. This forecast was governed by special rules. For example, the OMB director's economic assumptions (real growth, inflation, unemployment, and so on) had to be the same as those incorporated in the OMB midsession review of the budget issued during the summer. In the likely event that appropriations for the coming year had not been enacted, the forecast had to extrapolate the current year's spending (adjusted for inflation). Also, certain other rules had to be followed concerning entitlement programs, rates at which budget authority will be converted into spending, and so forth.

In the event a sequester had to be ordered, the director's initial report detailed the cuts that were to be made. By law, the sequester had to follow a strict formula. Some spending programs were exempt altogether, the largest two being Social Security and interest on the debt. Some other programs, such as Medicare, were partially exempt. Also, half the necessary outlay reductions had to be made in

---

[10] For example, President Bush's proposed budget for 1991 showed $1,233 billion in total spending—$753.3 billion from new budget authority and $480.0 billion from unspent budget authority enacted in earlier years (see *Budget of the United States Government, Fiscal Year 1991*, p. A-84).

[11] Of course, specific tax and entitlement programs may change, as existing law contains numerous provisions (previously enacted) that become effective according to a timetable.

domestic programs, half in defense programs. Because the rate at which budget authority is spent in defense programs is much slower than in domestic programs, the reduction in defense budget authority had to be much greater than the reduction in domestic budget authority.

The initial sequester order took effect on October 1, the beginning of the fiscal year. (That is, spending was withheld according to the plan set out in the initial sequester report.) But on October 15, the OMB director issued a final Gramm-Rudman-Hollings report reflecting congressional and presidential action at that point in time. Just as before, special rules had to be followed in determining the forecast. If at this time the deficit forecast exceeded the Gramm-Rudman-Hollings target by more than $10 billion, the president had to order sufficient spending resources sequestered to get the forecast down to the Gramm-Rudman-Hollings target.

The 1990 budget deal altered this procedure somewhat. If legislation resulted in an increase in the deficit (that is, spending in excess of the limits set out in the budget deal and/or a decrease in tax revenue), a sequester had to be ordered fifteen days after the end of a congressional session. In addition, sequesters had to be ordered within major discretionary spending categories—defense, international, and domestic—if the legislated levels exceeded those spelled out in the budget deal.

Under the 1990 act, each year the spending limits were adjusted for the updated economic assumptions contained in the president's January budget submission. Moreover, certain expenditures were excluded from the spending ceilings: Operation Desert Shield (Middle East), debt forgiveness to Egypt and Poland, funding for the International Monetary Fund, and emergency appropriations requested by the president. Estimates of losses stemming from defaults on new direct loans and new loan guarantees had to be appropriated and included in spending totals. Also, the Social Security surplus was excluded from calculations of the deficit.

The basic framework of spending controls is continued in the 1993 budget deal. However, the president has considerable latitude to impose these controls or not to impose them, depending on his assessment of the state of the economy and budget priorities. The budget deal also increased the statutory limit on the public debt from $4.4 trillion to $4.9 trillion—enough to accommodate government borrowing through 1995.

Even after the budget is "final," adjustments may be made to it. First, the president can ask for a *rescission*—that is, request that Congress pass a law reducing the amount appropriated for some program. Or the president can ask for a *supplemental*—an increase in spending for some particular program. Also, the president may ask for a change in the tax law—either increasing taxes or decreasing taxes. Of course, laws to change spending or revenues in a given fiscal year may originate with Congress itself. Although rescissions are frequently proposed, they are seldom approved. On the other hand, nearly every year Congress approves one or more emergency supplementals.[12]

Finally, something called the *current services baseline* (or simply *current services*) is widely used in budget discussions. Originally meant to be simply an adjustment of the previous year's spending and revenue levels to reflect inflation and so serve as a benchmark for new budget proposals, the current services budget now reflects many other adjustments that raise its levels (see discussion in text, especially chapter 10).

---

[12] Under Gramm-Rudman-Hollings, whenever Congress took any action during a fiscal year that would increase spending or reduce tax revenue (for example, approving a supplemental or granting a tax break) sufficient to raise the forecast above the deficit target, it is supposed to find offsets (for example, reducing spending in some other program or raising revenue from some other source) to avoid increasing the deficit.

Index